MICHAEL JOSEPH
AN IMPRINT OF
PENGUIN BOOKS

LUKE'S COOKBOOK

100 CLASSIC FAVOURITES
GIVEN A MODERN MAKEOVER
BY THE UK'S YOUNGEST HEAD CHEF

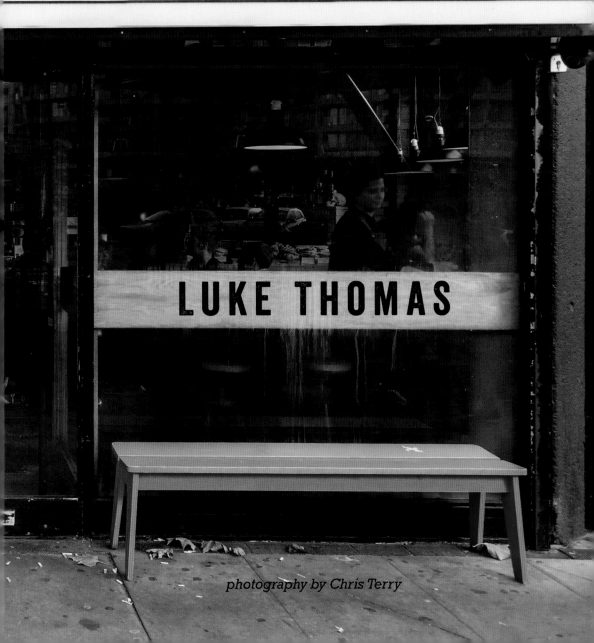

LUKE THOMAS

photography by Chris Terry

MICHAEL JOSEPH

Published by the Penguin Group
Penguin Books Ltd, 80 Strand, London WC2R 0RL, England
Penguin Group (USA) Inc., 375 Hudson Street, New York, New York 10014, USA
Penguin Group (Canada), 90 Eglinton Avenue East, Suite 700, Toronto, Ontario, Canada M4P 2Y3
(a division of Pearson Penguin Canada Inc.)
Penguin Ireland, 25 St Stephen's Green, Dublin 2, Ireland (a division of Penguin Books Ltd)
Penguin Group (Australia), 707 Collins Street, Melbourne, Victoria 3008, Australia
(a division of Pearson Australia Group Pty Ltd)
Penguin Books India Pvt Ltd, 11 Community Centre,
Panchsheel Park, New Delhi – 110 017, India
Penguin Group (NZ), 67 Apollo Drive, Rosedale, North Shore 0632,
New Zealand (a division of Pearson New Zealand Ltd)
Penguin Books (South Africa) (Pty) Ltd, Block D, Rosebank Office Park,
181 Jan Smuts Avenue, Parktown North, Gauteng 2193, South Africa

Penguin Books Ltd, Registered Offices: 80 Strand, London WC2R 0RL, England

www.penguin.com

www.lukethomas.co.uk

First published 2014
001

Text copyright © Luke Thomas, 2014
Photographs copyright © Chris Terry, 2014
Additional photography supplied by: Rick Barrett, copyright © Rick Barrett, page: 1
Alistair Richardson, copyright © Alistair Richardson, pages: 9, 241and 254–55
Every effort has been made to contact copyright holders. The publishers
will be glad to correct any errors or omissions in future editions.

Set in Rockwell, Veneer, Thirsty Rough, Bourbon and Veneer
Colour Reproduction by Tag: response
Printed in China

A CIP catalogue record for this book is available from the British Library

ISBN: 978–0–718–17886–4

★ CONTENTS ★

≡ INTRODUCTION ≡

My nan was the first person I ever cooked with. We used to grow our own vegetables in her garden, things like carrots, potatoes, cucumbers, tomatoes, lettuces, cabbages and strawberries. I really wanted to grow grapes, so I used to buy seeded grapes. I'd eat the grapes, keep the seeds, then bury them in a pot of earth and water them. The next morning, we'd rush out to the greenhouse and find grapes buried in the soil where the seeds had been! I think Nan had something to do with the grape-growing process though.

Nan loved cooking and she was quite traditional. Meat and two veg with gravy was pretty much her offering, and she taught me well. Cooking was my fun time. Our family didn't really go for convenience food, so we cooked from scratch every day. Mum was at work and she'd meet us at Nan's for our tea before taking me home for bedtime.

I remember when *The Naked Chef* started because Nan wouldn't let me see it as she thought it was a naked chef on TV. So, aged five, I used to sneak upstairs to watch it. What was exciting for me about Jamie Oliver was his freehand, easy approach to cooking, with no long lists of measurements to bog you down, which was way easier than following a recipe in a book. To me, a salad was tomatoes, lettuce and cucumber, and perhaps some celery, red onion and radishes. To Jamie, a salad had peaches, prosciutto, rocket leaves, fennel – all sorts of exciting ingredients that really got me thinking.

By the time I was twelve, it was clear that I was going to be a chef. My uncle arranged a day for me at the local butcher's, Steve Vaughan's, where I learned about making sausages, burgers, black pudding and basic butchery. I asked if I could come back and ended up working there for a couple of months. By the end, I was breaking down whole lambs into chops, legs, shoulders, racks and saddles.

When I started high school, my cookery teacher, Mary Richmond (Miss), noticed my huge love of food straight away. She took me to Soughton Hall, a local hotel and restaurant, where I met the head chef, Dan Hunter. Dan offered me work experience, which I think he intended to last a week, but two years later I was on the rota and a fully contributing member of their team. I would work most days after school and every weekend.

By then, I was reading everything I could about food, restaurants, food trends, international cuisines and famous chefs. Food was my life. I saved up my tips and took my mum and Miss to the chef's table at Claridges. It was my first Michelin star dining experience. I was absolutely amazed. The focus of the team, the level of service and their generosity left a huge impression on me. It made me wonder if they made all their guests feel this welcome. It's only after working in equivalent restaurants that I realized that this is the norm when you are cooking to this standard.

My next mission was to get myself behind the stoves in a Michelin-starred restaurant. The Chester Grosvenor offered me this chance. Simon Radley, their executive chef, took me under his wing. I remember my first task there on day one was to dice a pineapple. I thought, no problem! But on completing the task and having my entire effort thrown into the bin, I realized just how much I had to learn about cooking at this level. The chef took out a ruler and cut a perfect cube to make his point! I worked and trained there for two-and-a-half years.

Following eighteen months of further training and work experience, mostly with Iain Donald, a director of a large restaurant group, I met Mark Fuller who took a chance and gave me my first head chef position at Sanctum on the Green. I was eighteen years old and we called it Luke's Dining Room. I remember choosing the logo and sitting down to write the first menu and feeling so excited and proud. I had come a long way from planting grape seeds . . .

The last few years have been a bit of a rollercoaster for me. I wake up every day and can't believe how lucky I am, although it still seems crazy that I've written a book! My shelves at home are full of recipe books by my food idols and I can't believe that mine can now join them.

Looking back, there was a moment when, after a month cooking abroad, I returned to my nan's house and she made me a cup of PG Tips tea with a Mr Kipling cherry bakewell tart and I realized how comforting British food can be. It seems as though there's been a huge return to old-school eating – comforting pies, puddings and stews are now regulars once more on our menus. But I know it can get boring cooking the same thing again and again. So, this book is full of all those traditional dishes we remember from when we were children, but I've given them a bit of a twist for today's grown-up tables.

All the recipes are simple. There are no complicated preparation techniques and no ingredients you can't pick up at your regular supermarket. I love to have fun with food and I hate all the pressure people put on themselves when it comes to cooking and entertaining. I believe that eating together should be something to enjoy, not worry about. And just because you've been cooking your spag bol one way for years, doesn't mean you always have to. I've taken those classic recipes and given a new, fun spin to them.

I hope this book inspires you to play about with your cooking and have some fun with it, so that your everyday meals become something to celebrate. Life's too short to eat boring food!

Luke Thomas

MUSIC I LOVE TO COOK TO

CURTIS MAYFIELD MOVE ON UP
MADER DANCING IN THE MOONLIGHT
BASEMENT JAXX DO YOUR THING
KINGS OF LEON USE SOMEBODY
AMY WINEHOUSE VALERIE
DAFT PUNK GET LUCKY

CURTIS TOPLOADER
OASIS WONDERWALL
TRAIN DRIVE BY
THE KILLERS MR BRIGHTSIDE

CANAPÉS
& Cocktails

This chapter includes some of my favourite canapés and cocktails for getting a party going. If you have a group of friends coming round for a drinks party then this chapter has all you need to get organized. Choose a selection of nibbles, pair with a few of the retro-inspired cocktails and enjoy the evening!

I think setting the mood of a party is really important, and there's no better way to do it than through the food you serve. Everyone remembers the classic combination of cheese and pineapple on sticks stuck into a foil 'hedgehog'! But try my updated version of goat's cheese balls with a caramelized pineapple for a more modern take.

Pair your mini tasters with a choice of cocktails and mocktails. I've been lucky enough to work with some really amazing bartenders over the past year who know a thing or two about cocktails, so I've learned as much as I can about the perfect flavour blends and how to serve them with a flourish. I'm really grateful to Tom Rayfield who helped me design the cocktails and mocktails for Retro Feasts. I've included some of the most popular drinks that we had on the bar menu there and a few that I was inspired to create for this book. The sherbet lemon and raspberry ripple cocktails will give you a really retro start to the evening (they taste just like sweets!) and there are also a few delicious mocktails here so any non-drinkers don't feel left out.

All cocktail recipes serve one – they are easy to multiply up so you can make as many as you need. Alongside the nibbles here, you'll be the best host in town!

CANAPÉS

★ CHEESE AND PINEAPPLE ON STICKS ★

★ CHICKEN SATAY SKEWERS ★

★ DEVILS ON HORSEBACK ★

★ SMOKED SALMON BLINIS
WITH HORSERADISH CREAM ★

★ SHEPHERD'S PIE FRITTERS ★

★ FRESH SALMON VOL-AU-VENTS ★

MOCKTAILS

★ Orchard flower ★   ★ Pomegranate molasses ★

★ Sort of Shirley ★   ★ Virgin pina colada ★

COCKTAILS

★ Fruit salad ★   ★ Bacon bloody Mary ★

★ Raspberry ripple ★   ★ Englishman in New York ★

★ Retro Feasts' cheeky Vimto ★   ★ Sugar syrup ★

★ Peach snapper ★   ★ Sherbet lemon ★

★ Flowers of paradise ★

═ CHEESE AND PINEAPPLE ═
on sticks

MAKES 12   PREPARATION TIME: 5 MINUTES   COOKING TIME: 7 MINUTES

A spiky hedgehog made from half a grapefruit studded with cheese and pineapple on sticks was once the height of sophistication. I've given these classic party nibbles a bit of an update with sweet and juicy caramelized pineapple pieces and smooth and creamy goat's cheese balls. Hedgehog grapefruit, optional.

100g goat's cheese
¼ fresh pineapple, peeled
50g plain flour
1 egg, beaten
100g fine breadcrumbs

1 tablespoon vegetable oil
1 teaspoon coriander seeds
1 tablespoon icing sugar

12 cocktail sticks

Mould the goat's cheese into 12 balls, each roughly the size of a cherry tomato.

Cut the pineapple into 12 pieces, about the same size as the balls of cheese.

Tip the flour into a shallow bowl, the egg into another bowl and the breadcrumbs into a third. Roll the cheese balls first in the flour, then in the egg and finally in the breadcrumbs, pressing the crumbs firmly into the cheese.

Heat the vegetable oil in a frying pan over a medium heat and cook the breaded cheese balls for 3–4 minutes, rolling them around the pan so they brown and crisp up all over. Drain on some kitchen roll. Preheat the grill to hot.

Crush the coriander seeds in a pestle and mortar. Arrange the pineapple pieces on a baking tray, dust with the icing sugar and sprinkle over the coriander seeds. Grill for 2 minutes, until the sugar has caramelized and the seeds have started to smell very aromatic.

Skewer a piece of pineapple followed by a piece of cheese with the cocktail sticks. Serve while still a little warm.

CHICKEN SATAY SKEWERS

MAKES 12   PREPARATION TIME: 15 MINUTES   CHILLING TIME: 30 MINUTES
COOKING TIME: 15 MINUTES

These are ridiculously moreish, so beware! Thankfully, they're not as sickly as the classic version because of the fresh lime and chilli garnish, so you'll be able to eat more of them.

2 x 130g skinless chicken breasts
zest of 1 lime
1 fresh red chilli, very finely chopped
3 spring onions, thinly sliced
a few fresh coriander leaves

for the marinade
2 garlic cloves
zest and juice of 2 limes
1 tablespoon honey
1 tablespoon soy sauce
1 tablespoon smooth peanut butter

for the dipping sauce
1 onion, peeled and minced
1 tablespoon chilli flakes
½ tablespoon vegetable oil
150g smooth peanut butter
100ml coconut milk
50ml water
1 teaspoon soft brown sugar

12 wooden skewers

Cut the chicken breasts almost through horizontally and open out like a book. Place the butterflied chicken breasts between sheets of clingfilm and roll the chicken out so it's just under 1cm thick. Cut each breast into 6 strips.

Mix together the ingredients for the marinade and drop the chicken into it. Make sure the chicken is fully coated, then leave to chill in the fridge for 30 minutes.

Meanwhile, soak the skewers in cold water. Combine the lime zest and chopped chilli in a small bowl and set aside.

Fry the onion and chilli flakes in the oil over a medium heat for 4–5 minutes, until the onion is very soft. Add the rest of the sauce ingredients, give it a good stir and then bring to the boil. Boil for about 2 minutes, or until it has thickened.

Preheat the grill to high. Thread a piece of the marinated chicken on to each soaked skewer and grill for 3–4 minutes on each side, until cooked through.

Serve the chicken skewers scattered with the lime, chilli, spring onion and coriander leaves, alongside the dipping sauce.

There is nothing better than a few cocktails and nibbles with good company. With a little time and forward planning, you can create and serve delicious drinks and tasty canapés that will really impress your friends.

DEVILS ON HORSEBACK

MAKES 16   PREPARATION TIME: 5 MINUTES   COOKING TIME: 5 MINUTES

These little bites are a classic combination of crisp, salty bacon and sweet, juicy prunes. They make a brilliant alternative to cocktail sausages on sticks and are not only delicious, but also really simple to make. You can easily double up the quantities depending on how many people you have coming over.

1 teaspoon English mustard
4 tablespoons mango chutney
16 ready-to-eat prunes, destoned

8 rashers of thin streaky bacon or pancetta, fat removed, halved lengthways
a pinch of cayenne pepper
16 cocktail sticks, soaked in water

Preheat the grill to medium. Mix the mustard with the mango chutney and carefully spoon it inside the prunes. Wrap each prune tightly in a piece of bacon, holding it together with a cocktail stick.

Place on a baking tray and grill for 4–5 minutes, turning them every minute or so, until the bacon crisps up on all sides.

When they are cooked, finish with a light dusting of cayenne pepper. Serve with a cocktail (see pages 30–38 for some ideas).

SMOKED SALMON BLINIS

with horseradish cream

MAKES 30 BITE-SIZED BLINIS   PREPARATION TIME: 15 MINUTES
RESTING TIME: 40 MINUTES   COOKING TIME: 10 MINUTES

The texture of these little pancakes is denser than the classic version because of the wholemeal flour. I think it works really well with the fiery horseradish cream, which provides a surprising hit to the taste buds.

180g smoked salmon, roughly
  chopped into strips
1 teaspoon chopped fresh dill
optional: 2 teaspoons fish eggs (e.g. trout
  or salmon – or caviar if you're feeling fancy)

for the blini batter
120ml milk
15g fresh yeast
1 teaspoon sugar
120g wholemeal flour
2 eggs, separated
60g butter

for the horseradish cream
1 tablespoon peeled and finely grated
  fresh horseradish root (or you can use
  2 tablespoons from a jar)
½ teaspoon Dijon mustard
½ tablespoon white wine vinegar
½ teaspoon sugar
80ml whipping cream
salt and pepper

First make your blini batter. In a small saucepan, gently warm the milk over a low to medium heat. Crumble in the yeast and add the sugar. Stir until completely dissolved.

Place the flour in a mixing bowl and make a well in the centre. Add the egg yolks and half of the yeasty milk mixture. Beat together with a whisk, then add the rest of the milk. Mix to form a thick batter.

Cover the bowl tightly with clingfilm and leave somewhere warm for about 40 minutes, until bubbles begin to form and the mixture looks like it's growing in volume.

Meanwhile, in a medium-sized bowl, mix together all the ingredients for the horseradish cream. Whisk until soft peaks form, then season, to taste, with salt and pepper. Chill in the fridge until ready to use.

In a clean bowl, whisk the egg whites until they have formed soft white peaks. Whisk just a small amount of the egg white into the blini batter to loosen it, then carefully fold in the rest using a spatula.

Heat a non-stick frying pan over a medium heat and add a small knob of butter. When it has melted, spoon little mounds of batter evenly into the pan.

When the tops of the pancakes are covered in little bubbles (after about 1½ minutes), flip them over and cook on the other side for another 1½ minutes. Transfer to a plate and cover with foil to keep them warm while you cook the rest.

Scrunch a piece of sliced smoked salmon on top of each pancake, top with some horseradish cream and sprinkle with chopped dill. Finish with a few salmon eggs, if you're out to impress.

SHEPHERD'S PIE FRITTERS

MAKES 18–20 SMALL CANAPÉS   PREPARATION TIME: 15 MINUTES
CHILLING TIME: 30 MINUTES   COOKING TIME: 1 HOUR

Trust me, these may sound a bit crazy, but they are so ridiculously tasty you will wonder why you've not thought of it before. Serve with HP brown sauce to dip.

60g butter

2 tablespoons olive oil

2 onions, peeled and cut into small dice

2 carrots, peeled and cut into very tiny dice

2 sticks of celery, cut into small dice

450g minced lamb

1 tablespoon finely chopped fresh
  oregano or marjoram

300ml chicken stock

1 teaspoon Worcestershire sauce

500g Maris Piper potatoes

80g plain flour

2 eggs, beaten

300g breadcrumbs, e.g. Japanese
  breadcrumbs

vegetable oil, for frying

salt and pepper

Heat the butter and olive oil in a saucepan over a medium heat and fry the onion, carrot and celery for 4–6 minutes, until they have softened and started to take on some colour.

Add the lamb and the oregano or marjoram and cook, stirring, until the lamb is brown all over. Season with salt and pepper, then pour in the stock. Bring to the boil, then reduce the heat and leave to simmer for 20–30 minutes, stirring every so often.

Splash in the Worcestershire sauce and check the seasoning. The finished mince mixture mustn't be at all wet, as it will need to be held together with mashed potato. If it's still a bit liquidy, turn up the heat and let it bubble away for a few minutes. Set aside and leave to cool.

While it's cooling, place the potatoes in a large pan of salted water and boil for 15–20 minutes, until tender. Drain and mash until smooth.

Mix the hot mashed potato through the cold minced lamb until fully combined. Check the seasoning one more time before rolling into balls about 3cm in diameter.

Tip the flour into a shallow bowl, the beaten egg into another and the breadcrumbs into a third. Coat the shaped balls first in the flour, shaking off any excess, then coat in the egg and finally in the breadcrumbs. Chill in the fridge for 30 minutes.

Heat the oil in a deep-fat fryer to 180°C. (Alternatively, pour the oil into a large, deep pan set over a medium heat). Cook the balls in batches of three or four for about 2–3 minutes, until golden brown and hot all the way through. Leave to cool slightly before serving with HP brown sauce.

FRESH SALMON VOL-AU-VENTS

MAKES 30   PREPARATION TIME: 20 MINUTES   COOKING TIME: 30 MINUTES

These tasty mouthfuls were massively popular in the 60s and 70s. Personally, I've never been a fan of the originals; I think the traditional salmon mousse is too rich and creamy. But these little warm pastry puffs have a fresh salmon filling. Lovely.

500g ready-made puff pastry
plain flour, for dusting
1 egg, beaten
butter, for greasing
for the salmon filling
300g salmon fillets (skin on)
1 lemon, halved

5 black peppercorns
1 bay leaf
2 tablespoons chopped fresh parsley, stalks and leaves separated
2 tablespoons crème fraîche
1 teaspoon fresh dill, picked
salt and pepper

Place the salmon in a saucepan and squeeze over one of the lemon halves. Add the lemon shell to the pan. Cover with water and season with a little salt. Add the peppercorns, bay leaf and parsley stalks. Bring to a gentle simmer and cook for 8–10 minutes, until the fish is opaque and cooked through. Remove the fish from the water and leave to cool.

Meanwhile, make a start on the pastry cases. Preheat the oven to 180°C. Roll out the puff pastry on a lightly floured work surface until it is about 1cm thick. Using a 3cm-round biscuit cutter (or the rim of a small glass), cut out 30 pastry circles and lay them on a baking tray – leave a little space around each one. Lightly press a smaller biscuit cutter into the surface of each pastry round. (This will be the lid of the vol-au-vent once they are cooked.) Brush the discs with the beaten egg and bake for 15–20 minutes, until golden brown. Transfer to a wire rack and leave to cool a little.

When the fish has cooled, remove the skin and flake the flesh into a bowl. Mix in the crème fraîche, the parsley leaves, the dill and the juice from the remaining lemon half, leaving a little dill for garnishing. Taste, and season with a little black pepper. Set aside until needed.

When the pastry cases are cool enough to handle, carefully prise off the lids and make a hole in the bases by removing a few layers of pastry.

Spoon a teaspoon of the filling mixture inside each one and top with a sprig of dill.

TIP: *You can serve these as a starter. Just cut out larger pastry circles and fill with more of the delicious filling.*

≡ MOCKTAILS ≡

≡ *Orchard flower* ≡

The perfect drink for getting those non-drinkers in the mood for a party. You can mix everything apart from the soda in a big jug and keep it at the ready for quick and easy refills. Just make sure you give it a really good stir to break down the mint and release all that lovely fresh flavour and add a splash of cold water to get the same dilution as shaking it over ice.

Pour 35ml apple juice and 35ml elderflower cordial into a cocktail shaker. Place 10 large mint leaves in your hand and clap your hands together firmly to bruise the leaves and release their oils. Add to the shaker. Give it your best shake for 2 minutes, then strain into a martini glass. Top up with a splash of soda.

Clap another mint leaf between your hands, make a small tear on one side and pop it on the edge of the glass. This will give you a lovely hit of mint when you go in for a sip.

⟩ Sort of Shirley ⟨

Based on a classic Shirley Temple, this uses pomegranate molasses as a tangy, flavoursome replacement for the sweetness of grenadine. With the added heat of a good ginger beer, this is a drivers' drink that packs a punch. You can buy pomegranate molasses, but it's easy to make your own (see recipe below).

Pour 25ml pomegranate molasses and 25ml orange juice into a tall glass and add a few ice cubes. Slowly pour over some ginger beer right to the top. Garnish with a slice of orange on the side and a cocktail cherry. This is a drink that deserves two straws.

⟩ Pomegranate molasses ⟨

Put 1 litre pomegranate juice, 150ml lemon juice and 125g sugar into a pan set over a high heat. Bring to the boil, lower the heat slightly and simmer for about 30 minutes, until reduced by three-quarters. You should be left with a very sticky syrup.

⟩ Virgin pina colada ⟨

Coconut water is fresh, light and very healthy. In this extremely virtuous mocktail, the coconut milk gives a nice creamy texture, making it a more authentic pina colada, but you can replace it with an extra 15ml of coconut water if you prefer.

Pour 65ml coconut water, 65ml pineapple juice, 20ml lime juice, 25ml vanilla syrup and 15ml coconut milk into a cocktail shaker and give it a good shake for about 1½ minutes. Serve over ice in a tall glass. If you're feeling extravagant, garnish with 2 pineapple leaves.

COCKTAILS

Fruit salad

This cocktail is based on the flavours of the classic pink and orange chewy sweets, and the raspberry jam adds an extra stickiness, which creates that feeling of your teeth sticking together as you munch your way through a bag of sweets! For an extra retro feel, why not stick a sweet on top instead of the fruit garnish! Sugar syrup is now available in most supermarkets – look near where they keep their spirits – but it is really easy to make at home (see recipe below).

Pour 35ml Belvedere Black Raspberry, 15ml sloe gin, 15ml lemon juice, 50ml pineapple juice, 1 teaspoon raspberry jam and 1 teaspoon plain sugar syrup (see recipe on page 38) into a cocktail shaker. Give it a quick stir to dissolve the jam, then pop in a few ice cubes and shake vigorously for 1½ minutes. Strain into a short glass full of ice – you should get a nice foam on top. Skewer 2 raspberries and a piece of pineapple with a cocktail stick for a garnish. Use 2 short straws to slurp this one down.

Raspberry ripple

Who needs to eat dessert when you can drink it? This tastes exactly like every-one's childhood favourite ice cream! A great drink to serve after dinner, when everyone is too full to eat any more, but still wants a little something sweet.

In a short glass, mix 30ml raspberry liqueur and 15ml vanilla syrup, then fill with ice. Pour 35ml vanilla vodka and 50ml milk into a cocktail shaker and give it a vigorous shake for about 1½ minutes. Strain into the glass and garnish with 2 fresh raspberries and 2 straws.

Retro Feasts' cheeky Vimto

This is my favourite drink from the menu at Retro Feasts and is included here just because I love it! It's based on a classic nightclub 'cocktail' made from a blue alcopop mixed with a measure of port. We've changed it around, using a white port as the base of the drink and then topping it up with a raspberry liqueur. White port is made in the same way as the more traditional red version, but uses white grapes. For the best results, try to get hold of a young, dry style if possible – I recommend Dow's Fine White Port.

Pour 35ml white port, 25ml blue Curaçao, 25ml lemon juice and 15ml lime juice into a cocktail shaker, then strain into a large glass over crushed ice. Slowly pour 25ml raspberry liqueur over the top and it will start to sink . . .

Peach snapper

This is a great twist on a classic Bellini or a Kir Royale. It's perfect with a few nibbles at a party or while you're waiting for the barbecue to heat up – or just about any time, really. Creating the separate layers is really easy, but it's just to make it look good, so don't bother if you don't want the extra effort!

Shake 20ml peach schnapps, 10ml lemon vodka, 1 teaspoon sugar and 10ml lemon juice in a cocktail shaker for about 1½ minutes, then strain into a Champagne flute. To create a layered effect, slowly pour chilled Prosecco down a long spoon on to the surface of the peachy liquid. Garnish with a twist of lemon peel.

Flowers of paradise

This is a long and refreshing drink that makes a perfect pairing with charred meat.

Pour 35ml light rum, 35ml St-Germain Elderflower liqueur, 15ml lemon juice, 75ml grapefruit juice and 2 dashes of Angostura bitters into a cocktail shaker and give it a good shake for 1½ minutes. Strain into a tall glass over plenty of ice and top up with 35ml soda.

⬥ Bacon bloody Mary ⬥

This is quite possibly the world's greatest hangover cure: it is spicy, salty and has just enough booze to sort out your sore head! It's not just for hangovers, though – I like to serve these when I have people round for lunch. Keep a bottle of spice mix in the fridge and you'll be ready at a moment's notice! (Plus, you can use it to add flavour to loads of meaty dishes: stews, Bolognese or even as a marinade.) The bacon vodka takes a bit of planning if you can't find some in the shops. But it keeps for ever, so make a couple of batches and you'll never have to worry about it again.

Put some ice in a tall glass, then pour in 50ml bacon vodka (see recipe below), 35ml spice mix (see recipe below), an optional dash of fino sherry and a splash of Tabasco sauce, to taste. Top up with tomato juice and either a wedge of lime or a slice of very crispy streaky bacon to garnish!

for the bacon vodka

Cut the fat off 250g bacon (as fatty as possible), leaving as little meat attached as possible. It's the fat that you want in this recipe. Fry the fat in a pan over a low to medium heat, stirring regularly to make sure it doesn't catch and burn. It will take about 25 minutes for all the fat to melt. Pour a little vodka out of a 700ml bottle and strain the bacon fat into the bottle. Keep the bottle in a warm place for about a week before using, giving it an occasional shake. After a week, strain the vodka through a piece of muslin to get out all the fat solids. Rinse the bottle with very hot water, and then pour the bacon vodka back in! It will keep for ever.

for the spice mix

Mix 35ml lime juice, 20g sugar, 2 teaspoons smoked paprika, 2 teaspoons paprika, 2 teaspoons English mustard, 2 teaspoons hot horseradish sauce, 2 tablespoons sweet chilli sauce, 2 tablespoons tomato ketchup, 35ml balsamic vinegar and 290ml (1 bottle) Worcestershire sauce together really well, then strain into a bottle with a tight lid. Store it in the fridge and use it whenever you need a bit of spice in your life.

⚓ *Englishman in New York* ⚓

This is what Don Draper would be drinking if he lived in an East London loft apartment and rode a fixed-gear bike. Based on a classic Manhattan, but heavy on the vermouth and topped with a splash of pale ale for additional fruity, hoppy, bitterness. As this is slightly less punchy than the classic version, it's one to drink all day long.

Fill a tumbler with ice and pour over 35ml Scotch whisky, 25ml Martini Rosso and 2 dashes orange or Angostura bitters. Give it a stir, then top up with 50ml IPA or pale ale. Garnish with a slice of orange peel.

≋ *Sugar syrup* ≋

All sorts of flavours can be added to this basic recipe – I've tried pink peppercorns, fresh herbs or, for a great gingerbread syrup, ginger paste and a cinnamon stick. Just be sure to keep tasting to check the balance of flavour and sweetness. The plain syrup will keep indefinitely and the flavours will last for at least 2 weeks.

Simply pour 500ml water into a saucepan and add 300g granulated sugar. Heat over a low to medium heat until the sugar has completely dissolved.

For vanilla syrup, add the seeds of 2 vanilla pods to the pan as the sugar dissolves. You'll be able to see the seeds in the finished cocktails.

≋ *Sherbet lemon* ≋

This is a really refreshing drink, perfect on a summer's day by the barbecue. You can give this a bit of a fizz by topping up with soda and sprinkling over a little sherbet. Make a big batch to keep the crowd happy.

Pour 50ml lemon vodka, 50ml lemon juice, 20ml limoncello and 25ml sugar syrup (see above) into a cocktail shaker and give it a vigorous shake for about 1½ minutes. Strain into a tumbler over crushed ice.

SNACKS
& Starters

This chapter includes some great starters which can be eaten as snacks and light lunches, or simple suppers as well. One of my favourites is the Heinz-style tomato soup, especially when served in retro-style tins for a fun twist. A few of the recipes can also be downsized and served as canapés as well, like the crayfish cocktail – perfect bites in small lettuce leaves – or the crab on toast.

- ★ CHEESE TOASTIES ★
- ★ CRAYFISH COCKTAIL WITH MARIE ROSE SAUCE ★
- ★ MINI MIXED CHEESE QUICHES ★
- ★ CHICKEN COBB SALAD WITH BACON BITS ★
- ★ CRISPY DUCK SALAD ★
- ★ CHAR-GRILLED LETTUCE SALAD WITH ASPARAGUS AND BLACK PUDDING ★
- ★ CRAB ON TOAST WITH CRUSHED AVOCADO, CHILLI AND FENNEL ★
- ★ HEINZ-STYLE TOMATO SOUP ★
- ★ CHICKEN AND SWEETCORN SOUP ★
- ★ CHOWDER WITH BACON CRISPS ★

 CHEESE TOASTIES

SERVES 6–8 AS A TASTER   PREPARATION TIME: 5 MINUTES   COOKING TIME: 5 MINUTES

Hot little toasted cheese sandwiches are perfect with a cold drink – like one of the cocktails on pages 30–38. Cut the toasties into small triangles for the ultimate in retro finger food.

250g mature Cheddar cheese, grated
1 teaspoon English mustard
½ tablespoon Worcestershire sauce
3 drops of Tabasco sauce
1 egg yolk

optional: 1 tablespoon ale
10 slices of bread
1 tablespoon vegetable oil
salt and pepper

Mix together the cheese, mustard, sauces, egg yolk and ale (if using) in a bowl and season with salt and pepper.

Spoon on to 5 slices of bread and spread right up to the edges. Be careful when you spread it that you don't tear holes in the bread. Top with the other slices of bread to make 5 cheesy sandwiches.

If you are lucky enough to own a sandwich maker, then you'll know what to do next to make this ridiculously easy. Otherwise, heat the oil in a large frying pan over a medium heat and pan-fry the toasties for 1½ minutes each side, until the bread is lightly toasted and the cheese has melted and is starting to ooze out the sides. Make sure the oil doesn't get too hot as the bread can easily burn. Cut into small, bite-sized pieces.

CRAYFISH COCKTAIL
with Marie Rose sauce

SERVES 4   PREPARATION TIME: 20 MINUTES

It wouldn't be a retro feast without a prawn cocktail! I've updated the classic recipe using crayfish instead of prawns (but you can use prawns if you'd prefer to be more traditional!) and served it in lettuce leaves so you can eat it with your hands. The salad is lovely and fresh and crunchy, with the addition of apple and some sliced radish. I like *a lot* of Marie Rose sauce, but use as much as you like and serve the rest on the side to drizzle over the top.

½ cucumber, peeled, halved lengthways, deseeded and finely sliced

2 vine-ripened tomatoes, deseeded and diced

1 iceberg lettuce, 4 good leaves reserved, the rest finely shredded

40 cooked and peeled crayfish tails

1 Granny Smith apple, peeled, cored and chopped into matchsticks

4 radishes, finely sliced

1 box of cress

a pinch of cayenne pepper

for the Marie Rose sauce

180g mayonnaise

3 tablespoons tomato ketchup

a good pinch of cayenne pepper

a few drops of Tabasco sauce, to taste

1½ teaspoons Worcestershire sauce

Combine all the ingredients for the sauce in a small bowl. Taste, and add more Tabasco or Worcestershire sauce if you think it needs it.

Mix together the cucumber, tomato, shredded lettuce and crayfish with the Marie Rose sauce. It should coat all the ingredients evenly.

Arrange the 4 lettuce leaves on a platter and spoon crayfish cocktail into each one. Scatter over the apple, radish and cress and sprinkle with a little cayenne pepper.

Pick them up and eat with your hands – have some fun with your crayfish cocktail!

My fantastic team of chefs at Retro Feasts

MINI MIXED CHEESE QUICHES

MAKES 6   PREPARATION TIME: 30 MINUTES
CHILLING TIME: 50 MINUTES   COOKING TIME: 55 MINUTES

Impress everyone with your pastry skills by making these little tarts. Don't be put off by what you've heard – it's not difficult. If you really can't be bothered, you can cheat and buy some ready-made pastry, although you'll miss out on the extra cheesy flavour (you will need 500g ready-made shortcrust pastry to make six individual tarts). My aunty used to make cheesy quiches whenever she had a party, and I loved them! If you're having one of these for lunch, eat it with a salad and some baked beans. Amazing.

100g blue cheese, crumbled
  (I like using Stilton or Roquefort)
200g mature Cheddar cheese, grated
1 onion, peeled and grated
100g sundried tomatoes in oil, drained
  and chopped
½ tablespoon chopped fresh thyme leaves
2 small eggs
125ml milk
pepper

for the pastry
300g plain flour
50g Parmesan cheese,
  finely grated
a pinch of salt
150g butter, cut into cubes
1 egg, whisked with a splash
  of water

6 x 12cm round tart tins

First make the pastry by sieving the flour into a bowl and adding the Parmesan cheese and salt. Drop in the cubes of butter and, using your fingertips, rub the butter into the flour and cheese until it forms small breadcrumbs. Don't overwork it as this will go on to produce a heavy dough. Make a well in the middle of the mixture and pour in 2½ tablespoons of water. Using your hands or a knife, start bringing the mixture together to form a dough. Don't worry if it's a little crumbly. If it seems dry, then splash on a little more water, but don't add too much. Once it has formed a smooth dough, wrap it in clingfilm and chill in the fridge for 30 minutes.

When your pastry dough is nice and chilled, remove it from the fridge and divide it into 3 pieces. Roll out each piece on a lightly floured surface to a thickness of about a pound coin (roughly 2mm). Using a small plate as a template, cut out 6 rounds (2 from each piece), each roughly 16cm in diameter (they will need to line the tart tins with excess hanging over the edge).

Line the tart tins, pressing the pastry into the base and up the sides of the tin to make sure there aren't any air pockets. The pastry should stand just a little above the side of each tin, so trim away any excess. Leave to chill in the fridge for 20 minutes. Preheat the oven to 160°C.

Prick the base of each tart case all over with a fork. Cut out a piece of baking paper, 10cm larger than the diameter of the tin. Crumple it up, then unfold it and use it to loosely line the base of the pastry case. Fill the paper with baking beans. Repeat with the other pastry-lined tins, then bake in the oven for 20 minutes, until the pastry is just firm and starting to brown.

Take out of the oven, remove the paper and baking beans and brush the partly baked pastry cases with egg wash. Return to the oven for 5 minutes, so that they form a lovely shiny glaze.

Meanwhile, combine the cheeses in a bowl with the onion, sundried tomatoes and thyme. Season with pepper, then crack in the eggs and pour in the milk. Use a wooden spoon to gently mix all the ingredients together.

Turn up the oven to 170°C. Spoon the cheese mixture into the glazed tart cases and tap them gently on the sides to form an even layer. Cook in the oven for 20–25 minutes, until the filling is just set, but still has a bit of a wobble and it is lightly browned on top.

Serve with a tomato and onion salad dressed with a splash of olive oil and balsamic vinegar, and enjoy!

CHICKEN COBB SALAD
with bacon bits

SERVES 4   PREPARATION TIME: 10 MINUTES   COOKING TIME: 10 MINUTES

This is my take on the classic American salad. I've added some watercress for a bit of a peppery bite and you can use any blue cheese you fancy. It's great as a starter, but it could easily serve two people for lunch or as a light late-night dinner – which is apparently how it came about in the first place when a chef threw together a load of old leftovers and smothered them in dressing!

2 eggs
2 vine-ripened tomatoes
2 skinless chicken breasts
1 tablespoon olive oil
200g bacon pieces
1 iceberg lettuce, chopped into chunky 2.5cm pieces
1 avocado, peeled, stone removed, cut into small pieces
100g Roquefort cheese, crumbled

a small bunch of watercress, picked into small pieces

for the red wine vinaigrette
1 teaspoon Dijon mustard
1 teaspoon honey
1 tablespoon red wine vinegar
4 tablespoons olive oil
a pinch of salt and pepper

Place the eggs in a pan of cold water. Bring to the boil, then set the timer for 3½ minutes. Remove the eggs and cool in a bowl of cold water. Peel and set aside.

Meanwhile, bring a small saucepan of water to the boil and blanch the tomatoes for 30 seconds. Cool under cold running water, then peel off and discard the skins. Chop the tomato flesh into small pieces.

Cut the chicken breasts almost through horizontally and open out like a book.

Heat the oil in a griddle pan. When very hot, cook the butterflied chicken on one side for 3 minutes. Turn the chicken over and scatter around the bacon pieces. Cook for another 3 minutes on the other side, until the chicken is cooked through and the bacon has started to colour. Remove from the pan and cut each chicken breast into 6 pieces.

While the chicken and bacon are cooking, mix together the ingredients for the dressing.

In a large serving bowl, mix together the lettuce, tomato and avocado pieces, the crumbled Roquefort cheese and the cooked bacon pieces. Pour over the dressing and mix to coat. Quarter the soft-boiled eggs. Serve the salad scattered with the chicken and watercress and topped with the egg.

CRISPY DUCK SALAD

SERVES 4   PREPARATION TIME: 15 MINUTES   COOKING TIME: 1½ HOURS

This is, of course, inspired by the classic Chinese restaurant favourite: sweet, crispy duck, crunchy cucumber and sticky hoisin sauce all wrapped up in a floury pancake. Well, this salad contains all the flavours you love, with extra flashes of pink grapefruit balancing the heat of the dressing. Make sure you get plenty of that crispy skin through the salad for texture.

2 duck legs (skin on)

a drizzle of olive oil

salt and pepper

2 tablespoons toasted peanuts, chopped, to garnish

for the salad

1 small Chinese cabbage, chopped into rough 2.5cm chunks

2 red chicory heads, leaves separated

1 pink grapefruit, segmented

½ cucumber, cut into matchsticks

4 spring onions, finely sliced lengthways

1 red chilli, finely sliced (leave the seeds in if you like it hotter)

a large handful of bean sprouts

a handful of snow peas, shredded

1 tablespoon fresh mint leaves, torn

1 tablespoon fresh coriander leaves, torn

for the dressing

2 tablespoons soy sauce

1 tablespoon sesame oil

1 tablespoon olive oil

1 tablespoon honey

a pinch of dried chilli flakes

juice of 1 lime

2 teaspoons sesame seeds

Preheat the oven to 180°C. Place the duck legs in a roasting dish and drizzle with a little oil. Season with salt and pepper and cook in the oven for 1½ hours. The skin should be ridiculously crispy.

When it is cooked, shred the meat and skin off the bone using a couple of forks.

Gently toss together all the salad ingredients in a large serving bowl, then mix through the crispy duck and skin.

Put all the dressing ingredients in a jam jar with a lid and give it a good shake. Pour over the salad and mix lightly to coat.

CHAR-GRILLED LETTUCE SALAD
with asparagus and black pudding

SERVES 2, AS A LIGHT SUPPER   PREPARATION TIME: 5 MINUTES   COOKING TIME: 5–10 MINUTES

Cooking lettuce gives it a really interesting texture. Here it's char-grilled very lightly, so it just starts to caramelize underneath but stays crunchy in the middle. This is a great one-pan meal – and you can easily double up the ingredients for more people. The dressing is quite punchy, but you need it a bit fierce to cut through the richness of the black pudding and bring all the flavours together.

12 asparagus spears

2 eggs

2 thick slices of black pudding (about 50g)

olive oil

freshly ground black pepper

1 large Gem lettuce, cut into quarters, lengthways

a large handful of watercress

for the dressing

1 tablespoon Dijon mustard

1 tablespoon runny honey

1 tablespoon white wine vinegar

3 tablespoons olive oil

salt and freshly ground black pepper

Slice 8 of the asparagus spears in half, lengthways. Using a vegetable peeler, create asparagus shavings from the remaining 4 spears and set them aside for later.

Bring a small pan of water to the boil and gently poach the eggs. You want the yolks to be nice and runny.

Heat a griddle pan over a medium heat, drizzle the black pudding with a little oil and cook it for 2–3 minutes on each side, until cooked through and a little crunchy around the edges.

As soon as you put the black pudding on the griddle, drizzle the asparagus lengths with oil and season with black pepper. Add them to the griddle pan and cook for about 3–4 minutes until lightly browned and they have those lovely criss-cross markings. After a couple of minutes, drizzle the lettuce quarters with oil and place them cut-side down next to the asparagus. Cook for a few minutes, until the lettuce has started to wilt and colour on its cooked side but is still crunchy in the middle. For the dressing, place all the ingredients in a lidded jar and give it a good shake.

When everything is ready, arrange the char-grilled lettuce, the asparagus spears and shavings and the watercress on a large serving platter or board. Toss gently then crumble over the black pudding. Drizzle with dressing and top with the poached eggs.

CRAB ON TOAST
with crushed avocado, chilli and fennel

SERVES 4   PREPARATION TIME: 15 MINUTES   COOKING TIME: 2 MINUTES

You can upgrade a meal instantly with a glug of flavoured oil. Here I've used a garlic and herb oil. Simply drop a few peeled cloves of garlic and a couple of sprigs of rosemary and thyme into a bottle of olive oil and let the flavours work their magic. You can use it after a few hours, but the flavours will get more intense the longer you leave it. If you don't have time to make your own, you can buy some pretty good ones, or just rub your bread slices with a peeled clove of garlic and scatter over a few chopped herb leaves. This is a favourite at the restaurant.

4 thick slices of sourdough bread

garlic and herb olive oil, to drizzle (see above)

1 bulb of fennel, halved, core removed and finely sliced

extra virgin olive oil, to drizzle

a few fresh coriander leaves

for the crab

450g white crabmeat

3 tablespoons crème fraîche

juice of 1 lemon

1 tablespoon finely chopped fresh dill

for the crushed avocado

2 vine-ripened tomatoes, finely sliced

2 fresh red chillies, finely sliced (leave the seeds in or scrape them out depending on how you like it)

a few sprigs of fresh coriander

a pinch of salt

juice of ½ lime

3 ripe avocados, peeled, stones removed, roughly chopped

In a small bowl, mix together the crabmeat, crème fraîche and lemon juice. Stir in the dill, then set aside while you make the crushed avocado.

Using a pestle and mortar (or a food processor), pound the tomatoes, chillies (reserving a few slices for a garnish), coriander and salt to a fine paste. Loosen the mixture with the lime juice, then mix in the avocado. You want to keep it quite chunky, so don't over-mash.

Heat a griddle pan until hot. Drizzle your slices of sourdough with a good glug of flavoured oil and cook them for 1 minute on each side, until toasted and with nice griddle marks running across them. Spread the toast with the crushed avocado and top with the crab mixture.

Quickly dress the fennel with a little extra virgin olive oil and scatter over the crab with the coriander leaves and the reserved chilli.

HEINZ-STYLE TOMATO SOUP

SERVES 4–6   PREPARATION TIME: 10 MINUTES   COOKING TIME: 35 MINUTES

My grandma used to feed me a bowl of Heinz tomato soup whenever I went round to her house after school. I used to love it with toasted soldiers dipped in. This is a richer, creamier version, but it tastes just the same!

1kg vine-ripened tomatoes
50g butter
1 teaspoon olive oil
½ onion, peeled and chopped
2 garlic cloves, peeled and crushed
2 tablespoons tomato ketchup

1 stick of celery, chopped
3 sprigs of fresh thyme
250ml tomato juice
100ml double cream
salt and pepper

Cut the tomatoes in half and scoop the seeds and pulp into a sieve set over a bowl to collect the juices. Chop the tomato flesh fairly finely.

Heat the butter and the oil in a casserole over a medium heat and cook the onion and garlic for 5 minutes, until softened but not coloured. Add the tomatoes and their juices (throw out the seeds), the ketchup, celery, thyme and tomato juice and season with salt and pepper. Bring to the boil, then lower the heat and simmer for 20–30 minutes, until it has reduced by about two-thirds.

Pick out the pieces of celery and thyme, add the cream and blitz the soup in a blender until smooth. Pass the soup through a fine sieve into the cleaned pan, bring back up to a simmer and serve.

CHICKEN AND SWEETCORN SOUP

SERVES 6 AS A STARTER, 4 AS A MAIN COURSE
PREPARATION TIME: 5 MINUTES   COOKING TIME: 40–45 MINUTES

I love ordering this soup from the Chinese takeaway, but sometimes it can be a bit gloopy. This is my healthier, fresher version. I don't really like very spicy food, but use as much chilli as you dare ...

2 skinless chicken legs
1½ tablespoons cornflour
1 litre good-quality chicken stock
200g tinned sweetcorn, drained

3 spring onions, finely sliced
1 fresh red chilli, deseeded and finely sliced
1 tablespoon sesame seeds
salt and pepper

Preheat the oven to 200°C. Season the chicken legs generously with salt and pepper and place in a small ovenproof dish. Roast the chicken for 35–40 minutes, until cooked through and golden brown. Remove from the oven, then shred the chicken from the bone. Set aside and keep covered in foil.

Whisk the cornflour into 100ml of the stock. Bring the rest of the stock to a gentle simmer in a saucepan over a medium to high heat. Stir in the cornflour and stock mixture, then add the sweetcorn and cooked chicken. Lower the heat and simmer for 5 minutes.

Mix together the spring onions, chilli and sesame seeds. Serve the hot soup with the spring onion garnish sprinkled on top.

CHOWDER
with bacon crisps

SERVES 6 AS A STARTER, OR 4 AS A MAIN COURSE
PREPARATION TIME: 10 MINUTES   COOKING TIME: 50 MINUTES

This is a lighter version of a classic chowder, but if you want it to be a bit heartier and more like the original, stir in some more cream at the end. Make sure you use thin-cut bacon, as it will produce much crispier crisps.

10 rashers of thin-cut smoked streaky bacon
750ml vegetable stock
1 tablespoon vegetable oil
1 white onion, peeled and finely chopped
2 garlic cloves, peeled and finely chopped
2 large Maris Piper potatoes, peeled, halved and thinly sliced
250g smoked undyed haddock fillet, skin removed and cut into 2cm chunks

235g tinned sweetcorn, drained
250ml milk
90ml double cream
1 tablespoon chopped fresh parsley, to garnish
salt and pepper

First, make the bacon crisps. Preheat the oven to 180°C and line a baking tray with baking paper. Lay the rashers of bacon on the paper, trying not to let them touch each other. Top with another sheet of baking paper and weigh it down with another baking tray. Cook in the oven for 20 minutes, until the bacon rashers are cooked through and crispy. Transfer to some kitchen roll to soak up any excess fat and leave to cool while you make the rest of the chowder.

Pour the vegetable stock into a small pan and bring to a gentle simmer.

Meanwhile, heat the oil in a large saucepan over a medium heat. Add the onion and garlic and cook for about 4 minutes, until softened but not coloured.

Add the sliced potatoes and cook for 5 minutes until they are starting to soften. Pour in the hot stock and simmer for 8–10 minutes. Gently stir in the fish, sweetcorn and milk, then increase the heat and bring to the boil. As soon as it has boiled, lower the heat again and simmer for a further 8–10 minutes. Season, to taste, with salt and pepper (you may not need much salt as the fish will be quite salty).

Ladle into serving bowls, swirl through some cream, crumble over the crispy bacon and garnish with chopped parsley.

BURGERS
& Grills

This is a really relaxed chapter – and one of my favourites in the book. I think eating and entertaining should be all about hanging out with your mates and enjoying some great food. It shouldn't mean hours in the kitchen or getting stressed out about the perfect menu. Sometimes a really good burger or a juicy steak is all you need.

There are fanastic recipes here – check out my ultimate double cheese-burger in an English muffin, inspired by trips to McDonald's as a kid (mine is much more delicious though!). And once you've got the hang of that, have a go at some of my topping suggestions – I love the classic BLT made with sautéed lettuce. Delicious. I've also included quite a few sides and extras for you to try, so play around with different combinations until you find what works for you.

And who can resist the best retro snack of all: a fishfinger sandwich? This one is a luxury version though, made with lobster, obviously.

★ CLASSIC DOUBLE CHEESEBURGER ★

★ BIG BREAKFAST BURGER ★

★ VENISON BURGER WITH CUMBERLAND RELISH ★

RELISHES AND SAUCES

★ *Cumberland relish* ★

★ *Home-made fresh burger relish* ★

★ *Cucumber relish* ★

★ *Special burger sauce* ★

EXTRAS

★ *Chorizo-basted corn on the cob* ★

★ *Garlic mushrooms* ★

★ *Cabbage and apple slaw* ★

★ *Onion rings* ★

★ LOBSTER FISHFINGER SANDWICH ★

★ HOT DOGS THREE WAYS ★

★ *Barbecue sauce glaze and slaw* ★

★ *New Yorker onions with sweet mustard* ★

★ *Fiery chilli dawg* ★

★ CHICKEN SANDWICH WITH TARRAGON MAYO ★

★ BUTTERMILK CHICKEN ★

★ HONEY AND CINNAMON-GLAZED PORK RIBS ★

★ LUXURY STEAK WITH SPEEDY SEASONING ★

= CLASSIC =
DOUBLE CHEESEBURGER

MAKES 8 BURGERS (TO CREATE 4 DOUBLE CHEESEBURGERS)   PREPARATION TIME: 25 MINUTES
CHILLING TIME: 30 MINUTES   COOKING TIME: 5 MINUTES

Inspired by a fast food classic, but healthier and far more delicious. See over the page for other topping options – you really can put pretty much anything on top of a good burger!

1 x quantity of special burger sauce
  (see page 74)
4 English muffins
8 slices of American cheese (the plastic stuff)
2 shallots, peeled and very finely chopped
2 small gherkins, finely sliced

for the burgers
250g pork mince
1 shallot, peeled and minced
1 tablespoon Dijon mustard
2 tablespoons chopped fresh parsley
1 egg yolk
500g beef mince
2 tablespoons vegetable oil
salt and pepper

In a large bowl, combine the pork with the shallot, mustard, parsley and egg. Season with salt and pepper and then mix in the beef. This stops you overworking the beef, which could leave you with dry burgers.

Mould the mixture into 8 thin burgers (about 1cm thick). Put them on a plate and chill in the fridge for 30 minutes, to firm up. Make the special burger sauce by mixing the ingredients together in a bowl. (Place in fridge until ready to use.)

When you're ready to cook the burgers, heat your frying pan, griddle pan or barbecue until it's hot, hot, hot. Preheat the grill and get the muffins toasting. Brush the burgers with a little oil and cook them for 2 minutes on one side, then turn them over and cook for 2 minutes on the other side. They will be browned on the outside and a bit pink on the inside – not rare, just blushing.

To assemble, top a muffin base with a burger, a slice of beautiful plastic cheese, scatter over some shallots, then top with another burger and another slice of cheese. Finish with a big dollop of the special sauce, a few slices of gherkin and top with the muffin lid. Wrap it up in some paper and you'll never look at a McDonald's in the same way again.

BIG BREAKFAST BURGER

MAKES 6   PREPARATION TIME: 55 MINUTES (EXCLUDING BURGER-MAKING TIME)
COOKING TIME: 10 MINUTES

OK, so this might be a bit much for your average weekday breakfast, but it's great for a hangover on a Sunday – and it's even better with a bacon bloody Mary (see page 36)! With that winning combo inside you, you'll be back on it in no time.

6 x burgers (using the recipe on page 68)
4 tablespoons vegetable oil
12 rashers of streaky bacon
100g black pudding, thickly sliced
6 eggs

6 sesame seed burger buns
  or English muffins
6 slices of American cheese
  (or any cheese of your choice)

Preheat a griddle pan over a medium to high heat. When hot, brush the burgers with half the oil and cook them for 3–4 minutes on each side, until cooked to your liking. After the burgers have been cooking for a couple of minutes, add the bacon and slices of black pudding to the griddle pan and cook for about 5–6 minutes, turning halfway through. (If your griddle pan isn't big enough, you can pan-fry these in a little oil.)

Meanwhile, heat the remaining oil in a large frying pan over a medium to high heat. When hot, fry the eggs for 3–4 minutes (you may need to fry the eggs in batches; keep them on a plate covered in foil until needed).

To assemble your mighty breakfast, place a cooked burger on the base of a sesame seed bun, top with 2 slices of bacon, a slice of cheese and a fried egg. Crumble over some black pudding and dollop on any sauces you fancy (I like the fresh burger relish on page 74). Top with the bun lid and enjoy a great start to your day.

VENISON BURGER
with Cumberland relish

SERVES 4   PREPARATION TIME: 25 MINUTES
CHILLING TIME: 30 MINUTES   COOKING TIME: 25 MINUTES

Venison is really healthy because it's very low in fat, but this means you have to be careful that it doesn't dry out when it cooks, which is why I've added some pork fat. The Cumberland relish on the next page is full of warm wintry flavours that go well with the gamey meat, but feel free to play around with your own ideas for sauces – simple mustard works well too.

1 banana shallot, peeled and sliced into thin rings
1 tablespoon vegetable oil
4 brioche buns
4 small leaves of Little Gem lettuce
Cumberland relish (see opposite)

for the venison burgers
600g minced venison loin
300g minced venison shoulder
100g minced pork back fat
1 tablespoon vegetable oil
salt and pepper

Place both types of minced venison and the minced pork fat in a mixing bowl. Season with salt and pepper and mix together thoroughly using your hands or a wooden spoon. Divide into quarters and mould each portion into a burger shape. Place in the fridge for 30 minutes to firm up while you make the relish (see page 73).

Fry the shallot rings in the oil in a small pan over a medium heat for about 8–10 minutes, until they are a good golden-brown colour and starting to crisp up. Drain on a piece of kitchen roll and leave to one side.

Heat a griddle pan or barbecue until very hot. Brush the burgers with a little oil and cook for 2–3 minutes on each side for medium. When the burgers are cooked to your liking, remove from the heat and leave to rest for 3–4 minutes, covered in foil. This will make the meat nice and tender.

While the burgers are resting, toast the brioche buns under a hot grill or in a toaster.

To assemble, place a small spoonful of Cumberland relish on each bun base and top with a cooked burger, followed by a lettuce leaf and a few shallot rings. Serve with a bowl of the leftover relish alongside.

≣ Topping ideas ≣

Once you have the basic burger recipe mastered, play around with your toppings. Rather than make two slim burgers, shape the mixture into fatter ones – they will take a minute or two longer to cook. The recipe above easily makes six to eight good-sized burgers. Here are some of my favourite combinations:

★ **Classic BLT**
Fried crispy Parma ham, chopped sautéed lettuce and tomato (see page 175) and home-made cherry tomato salsa (see page 125).

★ **Americana**
Onion rings (see page 77) or New Yorker onions (see page 80) and a dollop of crumbled blue cheese mixed with mayonnaise.

★ **Chilli cheeseburger**
Fiery chilli (see page 80) with grated Cheddar cheese and jalapeños.

≣ RELISHES AND SAUCES ≣

≣ Cumberland relish ≣

SERVES 4   PREPARATION TIME: 15 MINUTES   COOKING TIME: 20 MINUTES

Use a sharp knife or a potato peeler to thinly pare the zest from an orange and a lemon, making sure you avoid the white pith. Cut the peelings into thin strips, place them in a small pan of water and bring to the boil. As soon as the water has boiled, strain through a sieve and discard the water. Repeat the boiling and straining process one more time.

Place 6 tablespoons redcurrant jelly and 70ml port in another saucepan and add the blanched peelings, 2 teaspoons grated root ginger and the juices of the orange and lemon. Bring to the boil and whisk together. Remove from the heat and stir in 1 teaspoon Dijon mustard. Allow to cool slightly, then add 200g fresh redcurrants.

☰ Cucumber relish ☰

SERVES 4   PREPARATION TIME: 5 MINUTES   CHILLING TIME: 1½ HOURS

In a bowl, combine 50ml olive oil, a tablespoon of wholegrain mustard, 1 tablespoon white wine vinegar and the juice of half a lemon. Mix everything together vigorously and then stir in half a cucumber, halved lengthways, seeds removed, and finely diced. Season, to taste, with salt and pepper. Cover and leave in the fridge so the flavours can mingle.

☰ Home-made fresh burger relish ☰

MAKES 350G   PREPARATION TIME: 5 MINUTES   CHILLING TIME: 1½ HOURS

This is quite a sweet, juicy relish that is great for a barbecue or on a picnic – you can even have it with the mini mixed cheese quiches on page 48. Make it a little ahead so the flavours can develop. You *can* eat it sooner, but it tastes better after a few hours.

In a medium bowl, mix together 200g firm vine-ripened tomatoes, quartered and finely diced, ½ red onion, peeled, halved and finely diced, 1 fresh red chilli, chopped finely, 1 tablespoon chopped fresh oregano, 1 tablespoon chopped fresh basil, 2 tablespoons caster sugar, 2 tablespoons white wine vinegar, the juice of 1 lime and a pinch of salt, until well combined. Leave in the fridge for about 1½ hours so that all the flavours can work into the tomatoes.

☰ Special burger sauce ☰

MAKES ENOUGH FOR 4 BURGERS   PREPARATION TIME: 30 SECONDS (IF THAT)

Tangy, but without being too sweet, this special burger sauce goes with anything (well, almost). Just make sure you mix it in equal quantities.

So easy: combine 200g firm vine-ripened tomatoes, quartered and finely diced, ½ red onion, peeled, halved and finely diced, 2 tablespoons mayonnaise, 2 tablespoons Dijon mustard and 2 tablespoons tomato ketchup in a bowl.

☰ Chorizo-basted corn on the cob ☰

SERVES 4   PREPARATION TIME: 5 MINUTES   COOKING TIME: 20 MINUTES

Liven up your corn on the cob with this sweet and spicy glaze. If you're cooking your corn on a barbecue, slowly baste the cobs all over with the sauce, turning regularly so they cook evenly.

Bring a large pan of salted water to the boil and blanch 4 corn cobs for 5 minutes, until just softened. Drain well. Meanwhile, heat 2 tablespoons olive oil in a large pan over a medium to high heat and fry 150g uncooked, diced chorizo sausage for 5 minutes until it releases its delicious oils and starts to take on some colour. Stir in 3 peeled and crushed garlic cloves and a small bunch of freshly picked thyme leaves and cook for a further 5 minutes to let the flavours infuse. Drain the corn cobs, tip them into the frying pan with 20g butter and baste with the cooking juices for 5 minutes, turning frequently so that they colour all over.

☰ Cabbage and apple slaw ☰

SERVES 4   PREPARATION TIME: 5 MINUTES   COOKING TIME: 20 MINUTES

I love coleslaw and I don't think a barbecue is complete without it. I smother it all over everything (and it's good with the fried buttermilk chicken on page 85 too!). This is a lighter slaw using fennel and a mustard mayonnaise.

1 small red cabbage, shredded, 1 small white cabbage, shredded, 1 bulb of fennel, halved, core removed and finely sliced (reserve the tops), 2 Granny Smith apples (unpeeled), grated, 150g sultanas, 2 tablespoons olive oil, 1 tablespoon Dijon mustard, 75g mayonnaise, juice of ½ lemon, salt and pepper

Put all the ingredients in a large bowl and give everything a good mix to fully combine and get coated in the dressing.

⫸ *Garlic mushrooms* ⫷

SERVES 4–6   PREPARATION TIME: 5 MINUTES   COOKING TIME: 20–40 MINUTES

This is an old-school starter that I've turned into a really delicious, fresh side. I like to use a mix of portobello, wild, chestnut and oyster mushrooms.

Preheat the oven to 180°C. Arrange 500g mixed mushrooms in a roasting tin, cutting them up if you'd like them smaller but keeping them roughly the same size as each other. Melt 100g butter in a large pan and when it starts to foam, add 4 peeled and crushed garlic cloves and cook for 1 minute. Stir in 1 tablespoon of roughly chopped fresh tarragon leaves and the zest and juice of 1 lemon and cook for 30 seconds. Pour the herby garlic butter over the mushrooms, mixing to coat, and season with salt and pepper. Cook in the oven for 20–40 minutes, depending on the size of the mushrooms. They should be tender and juicy.

TIP: *To turn this into a tasty snack, serve on toasted sourdough and pour over the cooking juices.*

≋ *Onion rings* ≋

SERVES 4–6   PREPARATION TIME: 5 MINUTES   COOKING TIME: 15 MINUTES

How many onion rings have you eaten that are just soggy, greasy batter covering an almost raw piece of onion? The secret is to cook the onion rings in hot water for a bit beforehand so that they soften up. Then they don't need as long in the hot oil and you'll end up with the perfect crunch! These have some chilli flakes in the batter for a bit of heat, but you can leave them out, or use dried herbs instead.

In a large bowl, mix together 250ml lager and 150g plain flour and season with salt, pepper and chilli flakes, if using. The batter should have a fairly thick consistency and coat the back of the spoon. Add another 50g of flour if it seems a little thin. Set aside. Bring a large pan of salted water to the boil over a medium heat. Peel and slice 3 white onions into 1cm-thick slices. Remove and discard the inner rings and separate out the larger rings. Place the large onion rings in the boiling water and cook for 4–5 minutes until softened slightly. Drain, pat dry, then dust them in flour. Dip them straight into the batter to fully coat.

Pour vegetable oil into a large pan to a depth of about 10cm and heat to 190°C (test the temperature using a kitchen thermometer or drop a small cube of bread into the hot oil; the bread should bubble and turn brown in about 30 seconds). When the oil is hot enough, carefully drop in a few of the battered onion rings and cook for 3–4 minutes until golden brown and crispy. Use a slotted spoon to remove them from the oil and drain on some kitchen roll. Do not overcrowd the pan as this will reduce the temperature of the oil, resulting in soggy batter and uncooked onions.

LOBSTER FISHFINGER SANDWICH

SERVES 4   PREPARATION TIME: 25 MINUTES   CHILLING TIME: 1 HOUR   COOKING TIME: 20 MINUTES

This goes down a storm with everyone I make it for. There's something so comforting and satisfying about the combination of warm, sweet lobster and soft English muffin. Lobster may seem rather an extravagance, but you don't need a lot to serve four people. If you prefer, you can use white crabmeat instead.

450g Desiree or Maris Piper potatoes, peeled and cut into even-sized pieces
25g butter, plus extra to spread on the English muffins
200g cooked lobster meat, flaked
1 tablespoon Dijon mustard
1 tablespoon chopped fresh chives
juice of ½ lemon

cucumber relish (see page 74)
100g plain flour, seasoned with salt and pepper
2 eggs, beaten
100g breadcrumbs
vegetable oil, for frying
4 English muffins
8 small Little Gem lettuce leaves

First, make some mashed potatoes. Bring the potatoes to the boil over a medium heat and cook for about 15–20 minutes, until tender. Drain thoroughly, then return to the hot pan. Mash with the butter until smooth, but don't use any milk as the final mixture will be too wet. Leave to cool.

When the potatoes are cool enough to handle, gently mix them in a bowl with the lobster, Dijon mustard, chives and lemon juice. Season with a little salt and pepper.

Take a small handful of the lobster mixture and shape into a large 'finger'. Repeat so you end up with 8 lobster fingers. Place them on a plate and chill in the fridge for an hour.

While the lobster fingers are chilling, get started on the cucumber relish (see page 74).

When you're ready to cook the lobster fingers, line up 3 shallow bowls in front of you. Place the flour in one, the beaten eggs in another and the breadcrumbs in the third. Dip each lobster finger first in the flour, shaking off the excess, then in the egg and finally the breadcrumbs, so that they are fully coated on all sides.

Deep-fry the lobster fingers at 180°C for about 3–4 minutes, until the breadcrumbs are golden brown and crispy and the middle is piping hot – test by inserting a metal skewer, but be careful not to burn yourself. If you don't have a deep-fat fryer, shallow fry in a little oil for a couple of minutes on each side, until golden brown. Meanwhile, split open the muffins and get them toasting under the grill or in a toaster.

To serve, spread a little butter on each muffin, and top with 2 lettuce leaves, 2 lobster fingers and a generous spoonful of the cucumber relish.

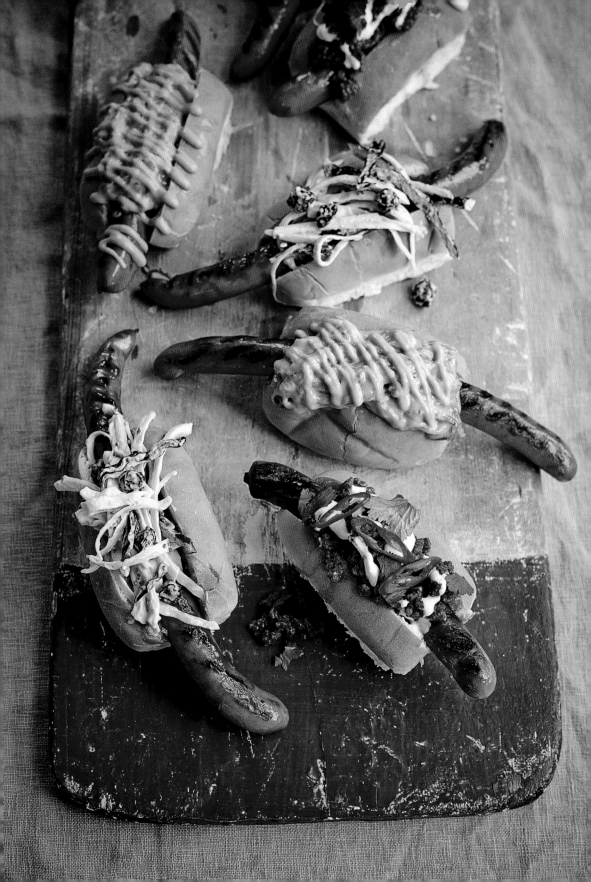

≡ HOT DOGS THREE WAYS ≡

Hot dogs are definitely a favourite meal from my childhood and I love that they're having a bit of a comeback! Buy good-quality wieners, serve them in squishy buns and smother them in one of these toppings. Char-grilling them for additional flavour will work really well.

≋ *Barbecue sauce glaze and slaw* ≋

PREPARATION TIME: 5 MINUTES   COOKING TIME: 10–12 MINUTES

Get a griddle pan really hot. Brush the hot dogs liberally with 2 tablespoons barbecue sauce and cook for 10–12 minutes, turning regularly until cooked through. Serve in a bun topped with cabbage and apple slaw (see page 75).

≋ *New Yorker onions with sweet mustard* ≋

PREPARATION TIME: 5 MINUTES   COOKING TIME: 40–50 MINUTES

In a large frying pan set over a low heat, very gently fry 3 peeled and sliced white onions in 2 tablespoons vegetable oil for 20 minutes. Stir in 2 tablespoons sugar and cook for a further 20–30 minutes. You want them to be really sticky and broken down.

Mix together 3 tablespoons mayonnaise and 3 tablespoons Dijon mustard, tasting and adding more mustard if you like.

Serve a generous amount of the sticky onions and drizzle with the sweet mustard.

≋ *Fiery chilli dawg* ≋

PREPARATION TIME: 10 MINUTES   COOKING TIME: 30 MINUTES

Heat 1 tablespoon vegetable oil in a saucepan over a medium heat and cook ½ peeled and minced onion, 1 peeled and crushed garlic clove, ½ teaspoon ground cumin and ½ teaspoon chilli powder for 4–5 minutes, until the onion is soft. Add 200g beef mince and cook for about 5 minutes, until browned all over.

Stir in 1 chopped tomato and 1 finely chopped fresh red chilli (reserving a little to garnish). Pour in 100ml water and simmer gently for 20 minutes. This should be quite a dry chilli, so leave it for a few more minutes if you think it needs it.

Top your dogs with a spoonful of the chilli, then dollop on some sour cream, a handful of chopped fresh coriander and the reserved chopped chilli.

CHICKEN SANDWICH
with tarragon mayo

SERVES 4   PREPARATION TIME: 30 MINUTES   MARINATING TIME: OVERNIGHT
COOKING TIME: 10 MINUTES

You'll need to get this one started the day before so that the marinade can really work into the meat to give you a lovely rich, lemony taste. The tarragon mayonnaise goes so well with it – make sure you really smother it on! To keep it looking fresh and green, only chop the tarragon once or twice.

2 lemons
a small bunch of fresh thyme
3 tablespoons olive oil, plus extra to drizzle
2 skinless chicken breasts
4 slices of sourdough bread

for the salad
a small bag of rocket
a handful of grated Parmesan cheese
1 tablespoon olive oil

for the tarragon mayonnaise
2 egg yolks
2 teaspoons Dijon mustard
2 tablespoons white wine vinegar
  (or tarragon vinegar if you can find it)
260ml olive oil or rapeseed oil
1 tablespoon chopped fresh tarragon
salt and black pepper

Squeeze the lemons into a shallow bowl and throw in the lemon shells too. Scatter over the thyme and pour in the olive oil. Mix to combine, then add the chicken and use your hands to work the marinade into the meat. Leave in the fridge overnight.

Make the mayonnaise by whisking together the egg yolks, mustard and vinegar, using an electric whisk on a medium speed for about 5 minutes, until it has increased in volume. Slowly add the oil, continuously whisking until completely incorporated and you have a good wobbly mayonnaise. Thin if needed with a little warm water. Season, to taste, with salt and pepper and then stir through the tarragon.

To cook the chicken, heat a griddle pan over a medium to high heat. Cut the chicken breasts through horizontally so you have 4 thin fillets. Cook the chicken for 2–3 minutes on each side, until cooked through. Transfer to a plate and cover with foil.

Drizzle the bread with a little oil and griddle for 2 minutes on each side until it is nicely char-grilled and has absorbed some of the cooking juices from the chicken. Meanwhile, toss together the salad ingredients.

Spread the tarragon mayo on to the toast, top with the chicken and scatter over a handful of the salad. Have the rest of the mayonnaise on the side.

BUTTERMILK CHICKEN

SERVES 4–6   PREPARATION TIME: 15 MINUTES
CHILLING TIME: 2 HOURS OR OVERNIGHT   COOKING TIME: 5 MINUTES

Buttermilk has a really distinct taste – it's almost slightly yeasty, which makes it a great addition to savoury dishes. You can use other chicken pieces here too; thighs and drumsticks will work well, just make sure they are properly cooked through.

600g chicken mini fillets
200g plain flour
½ teaspoon salt
½ teaspoon pepper
1 teaspoon paprika
1 tablespoon vegetable oil
a knob of butter
1 x quantity of cabbage and
  apple slaw (see page 75)

for the marinade
300ml buttermilk
2 teaspoons cayenne pepper
2 teaspoons Dijon mustard
1 teaspoon salt

Combine the ingredients for the buttermilk marinade in a large bowl. Drop in the chicken pieces, mix to coat, then cover with clingfilm and chill in the fridge for 2 hours (or overnight if you have the time).

Mix together the flour, salt, pepper and paprika in a shallow dish.

When you're ready to cook the chicken, heat the oil in a frying pan over a medium to high heat. Dip the chicken, piece by piece, in the flour, tapping off the excess, then place them straight in the hot pan. Cook for 1 minute, then turn them over and cook for another minute. Turn down the heat, add the butter and cook for a final minute, turning often. The chicken should be lovely and golden and a little crispy in places. Serve with the crunchy slaw.

HONEY AND CINNAMON-GLAZED PORK RIBS

SERVES 4   PREPARATION TIME: 30 MINUTES   CHILLING TIME: 12–24 HOURS
COOKING TIME: 2–2½ HOURS

These have a really intense flavour hit that comes from the dry spice rub, which you should rub into the ribs at least 12 hours before you cook them. So ridiculously tasty; just pile them up in the middle of the table and watch everyone get messy!

1 full rack of baby back pork ribs
250ml lager or beer
1 tablespoon dark molasses

for the spice rub
1 tablespoon ground cinnamon
1½ teaspoons sea salt
1½ teaspoons soft brown sugar

for the glaze
3 tablespoons clear honey
1 tablespoon tomato ketchup
1 teaspoon soy sauce

First make the spice rub by mixing together the cinnamon, salt and sugar. Rub the mixture all over the ribs, turning and working it into the meat so that the ribs are completely covered. Place the ribs in a baking dish, cover with foil and leave in the fridge for at least 12 hours and preferably 24 hours.

When you're ready to cook the ribs, preheat the oven to 250°C. Pour the lager or beer and the molasses around the ribs in the baking dish. Cover tightly with foil. Cook in the oven for 1–1½ hours, basting every 20 minutes. The meat should be lovely and tender and you should be able to insert a knife easily between the meat and the bone. Remove from the oven and keep covered. Lower the oven temperature to 180°C.

Mix together the glaze ingredients in a small heatproof bowl set over a pan of simmering water. Keep stirring for about 3–4 minutes.

Separate the ribs by cutting down between the bones with a sharp knife. Throw away the braising liquid. Arrange the ribs on a baking tray and paint them all over with the glaze. Cook in the oven for 45 minutes–1 hour so that they become caramelized and sticky.

LUXURY STEAK
with speedy seasoning

SERVES 4   PREPARATION TIME: 10 MINUTES   COOKING TIME: 10 MINUTES

Rib-eye steaks are, hands down, my favourite steaks. They can be cooked in almost any way and still stay juicy and tender. They are a bit more expensive than other cuts, but sometimes you just have to do it. This quick seasoning is so easy to make, but will give your steak the most amazing flavour.

4 x 12oz (340g) rib-eye steaks, each about 2cm thick
1 tablespoon vegetable oil
a bag of watercress, to serve

for the seasoning
1 shallot, peeled and very finely chopped
zest of 1 lemon
1 fresh red chilli, very finely chopped
2 garlic cloves, peeled and crushed
½ teaspoon salt
2 tablespoons olive oil
1 tablespoon chopped chives

Brush the oil all over the steaks and leave them on a plate to come up to room temperature.

Meanwhile, spread the seasoning ingredients all over a chopping board or across a couple of large plates.

Get your barbecue or griddle pan really hot. Cook the steaks for 3 minutes on one side until they start to colour, then flip them over and cook for 3 minutes on the other side. Flip the steaks back over again (ideally in the other direction to get good criss-cross markings) for a final 3 minutes.

When the steaks are cooked, immediately place them on top of the seasoning. Slice the meat, coating the steak as you carve. Transfer to plates and serve with the watercress and any cooking juices poured over the top.

Everybody has their favourite cut of steak, but there are some simple things to look for: a nice dry piece of meat with a good amount of marbling, as opposed to chunks of fat, because as the steak cooks the fat will render and give you a lovely flavour.

GROWN-UP
Dinners

During the week, no one can be bothered to cook anything too fancy. We all end up resorting to the same few dishes and I know it can get boring. In this chapter, I've taken those well-loved recipes and given them a bit of a twist to bring them up to date and add something new to your mealtimes. They're just simple extras – like a breadcrumb crust or a special sauce – but they will make all the difference to Tuesday night's dinner, without a load of extra hassle.

There are some great retro dinners in here that I remember from my childhood, like gammon, egg and pineapple and beans on toast, but they all have something a bit special going on. And give my spicy beef noodle pot a go! You'll never stop off at the takeaway again with this lot on the menu and it will make you look at your regular recipes in a whole new way!

- ★ CORONATION CHICKEN SALAD WITH CARAMELIZED ALMONDS ★
- ★ ROAST CHICKEN, VEGETABLE AND PASTA BAKE ★
- ★ CHICKEN BREASTS WRAPPED IN BACON ★
- ★ CHICKEN UNDER A BRICK ★
- ★ CALVES' LIVER AND BACON WITH MASH AND ONION GRAVY ★
- ★ SAUTÉED CHICKEN LIVERS WITH MARSALA, GRAPES AND SHALLOTS ON TOAST ★
- ★ HOME-MADE CORNED BEEF ★
- ★ CORNED BEEF HASH CAKES WITH FRIED EGGS ★
- ★ SPAGHETTI BOLOGNESE WITH A PARMESAN-HERB TOPPING ★
- ★ RUMP STEAK SUPPER WITH A MUSTARD AND PEPPERCORN CRUST AND INSTANT TOMATO RELISH ★
- ★ SPICY BEEF NOODLE POT ★

- ★ ROASTED COD IN PARSLEY SAUCE ★
- ★ SMOKED HADDOCK AND CRAB CAKES ★
- ★ FISH SUPPER ★
- ★ SMOKED HADDOCK SCOTCH EGG WITH CURRY MAYONNAISE ★
- ★ SARDINES 'ON TOAST' WITH CHERRY TOMATO SALSA ★
- ★ SAUSAGE ROLLS WITH CRACKED PINK PEPPERCORN SAUCE ★
- ★ GAMMON, EGG AND PINEAPPLE SALSA ★
- ★ PAN-FRIED PORK CHOPS WITH BLACK PUDDING CROQUETTES AND CIDER AND APPLE SAUCE ★
- ★ BREADED LAMB CUTLETS STUFFED WITH GOAT'S CHEESE ★
- ★ SHEPHERD'S PIE ★
- ★ MAC'N'CHEESE ★
- ★ BEANS ON TOAST ★
- ★ PEA AND GOAT'S CHEESE RISOTTO ★

CORONATION CHICKEN SALAD

with caramelized almonds

SERVES 4   PREPARATION TIME: 10 MINUTES   COOKING TIME: 25 MINUTES

I used to eat coronation chicken salad every Thursday after school when we went shopping, so this dish brings back some good memories! If you don't have time to caramelize your almonds, you can just use plain flaked ones instead, but I think that extra sweet crunch makes all the difference. The home-made mayonnaise on page 82 will be great here too (just leave out the tarragon).

400g cooked chicken, chopped or
shredded into bite-sized pieces

for the salad
1 stick of celery, chopped
2 spring onions, chopped
½ cucumber, halved lengthways
and chopped
a small bag of watercress

for the caramelized almonds
100g flaked almonds
2 tablespoons icing sugar

for the curry mayonnaise
225g mayonnaise
2 tablespoons raisins
½ fresh mango, peeled and
roughly chopped
3 teaspoons curry powder

First make the caramelized almonds. Preheat the oven to 180°C. Scatter the almonds on to a non-stick baking tray and sprinkle over the icing sugar. Give them a quick toss to coat, then cook in the hot oven for 20–25 minutes, until nicely caramelized and a bit sticky. Leave them to cool while you make the rest of the salad.

Combine the mayonnaise ingredients in a large bowl. Add the chicken and mix gently to coat in the curry sauce. Top with the almonds.

Toss together the chunky salad and serve with the chicken.

ROAST CHICKEN, VEGETABLE AND PASTA BAKE

SERVES 4   PREPARATION TIME: 20 MINUTES   COOKING TIME: 1 HOUR

This easy weeknight dinner is the perfect way to use up any leftovers from a Sunday roast. It's a real crowd pleaser and the ultimate in retro comfort food – and so much better than spooning it out of a jar of sauce.

400g macaroni, penne or fusilli
100g broccoli, cut into small florets
100g cauliflower, cut into small florets
600ml milk
60g butter
60g plain flour
200g Gruyère cheese, grated

250g Parmesan cheese, grated
250g roast chicken
60g pine nuts
4 spring onions, chopped
  (use the white and green parts)
salt and pepper

Bring a large pan of salted water to the boil and cook the pasta according to the packet instructions. It should be al dente. Drain, refresh under cold running water, then tip into a large bowl and set aside.

Meanwhile, in a separate pan of boiling salted water, cook the broccoli and cauliflower for about 5 minutes, until just tender. Drain, refresh under cold running water and add to the drained pasta.

In a small saucepan, bring the milk to the boil. At the same time, in a separate pan, melt the butter and stir in the flour until completely incorporated. With the pan still on the heat, pour the hot milk on to the flour mixture, a little at a time, whisking and stirring until you have a smooth, thick white sauce. Remove from the heat and add three-quarters of the Gruyère and Parmesan cheeses. Taste and season with a little salt and pepper if you think it needs it. Preheat the oven to 200°C.

Pour three-quarters of the cheese sauce over the pasta and vegetables. Flake the cooked chicken into the mix and add the pine nuts and spring onions.

Divide the mixture into four individual ovenproof dishes. Top up with the remaining cheese sauce and sprinkle over the remaining cheese. Bake for about 30 minutes until crusty and golden brown on top.

CHICKEN BREASTS WRAPPED IN BACON

SERVES 4   PREPARATION TIME: 15 MINUTES   COOKING TIME: 50 MINUTES

Chicken wrapped in bacon is a midweek regular in households up and down the country; it's easy, fairly inexpensive and comforting after a long day. Play around with different flavoured butters – see my suggestions at the end of the recipe.

8 slices of Parma ham
4 skinless chicken breasts, butterflied

4 tablespoons flavoured butter (see Tip)
1 tablespoon vegetable oil

Preheat the oven to 180°C. Tear off a 25cm x 25cm sheet of foil and place it on your work surface.

Cut the chicken breasts almost through horizontally and open out like a book.

Arrange 2 slices of Parma ham next to each other on top of the foil, followed by a chicken breast. Spread 1 tablespoon of flavoured butter all over the chicken.

Using the edge of the foil to help you, roll the ham and chicken over tightly and away from you. Keep rolling like you would a Swiss roll, keeping the foil on the outside. When you have finished, wrap the chicken up in the foil and twist the ends to seal it like a Christmas cracker. Repeat with the rest of the ham, chicken and butter.

Place the chicken parcels in a baking dish and cook in the oven for 45 minutes.

When the chicken cooking time is up, remove the chicken parcels from the oven and carefully unwrap them. Heat the oil in a frying pan over a medium to high heat and fry them for 5 minutes, turning often, to add some colour. Remove from the heat and slice thickly. Serve the chicken slices with some char-grilled asparagus dressed in olive oil or pan-fried Jersey Royals (see page 202) on the side.

TIP: *Flavoured butters can immediately upgrade any dish and they're really easy to make. Just mix together softened butter with your choice of flavourings. You can then roll the butter into a sausage shape, wrap it in greaseproof paper and freeze it. Simply slice off a round whenever you need to add some extra oomph! Here are three of my favourites:*

Quantities are for 250g butter ★ 1 tablespoon chopped fresh mixed herbs ★ 2 garlic cloves, peeled and crushed, mixed with 1 teaspoon chilli flakes ★ 2 anchovies, chopped very finely, mixed with 2 teaspoons fresh rosemary leaves

CALVES' LIVER AND BACON
with mash and onion gravy

SERVES 4   PREPARATION TIME: 10 MINUTES   COOKING TIME: 35 MINUTES

What's more retro than liver and bacon? Maybe onion gravy? Here you've got them all, with a rich and creamy mash to mop it all up.

500g Maris Piper potatoes, peeled and halved
150ml milk
50g butter
1 tablespoon vegetable oil
4 x 150g calves' livers
salt and pepper

for the onion gravy
1 tablespoon vegetable oil
100g bacon pieces or cubes of pancetta
1 red onion, peeled and grated
a small bunch of fresh sage
150ml red wine
300ml hot chicken stock
1 tablespoon brandy
1 tablespoon redcurrant jelly

First make the mash. Place the potatoes in a large pan of salted water and bring to the boil. Cook for 15–20 minutes, until tender when poked with a fork. Drain and mash with the milk and butter until very smooth. Season with pepper and a little salt, then cover with the lid to keep it warm.

Heat the oil in a large frying pan over a medium to high heat. Cook the livers for 2 minutes on one side, then turn them over and cook for 1 minute on the other side. Transfer to a plate and season with salt and pepper.

Keeping the pan on the heat, add the oil for the onion gravy. Fry the bacon until it starts to brown and has released some of its fat. Stir in the grated onion and cook for about 5 minutes, until softened and starting to colour and caramelize. Add the bunch of sage, pour in the wine and simmer until it has reduced by about two-thirds. Add the hot stock, turn up the heat a little, then leave it bubbling away until it has reduced by about half. Remove the sage and stir in the brandy and redcurrant jelly.

Return the liver to the pan, coat in gravy and cook for 1 minute. Serve immediately with the mash to one side and the gravy poured over the top.

TIP: *To get extra-smooth mashed potatoes, heat the milk with the butter in a small sauce-pan on the hob until the butter has completely melted before using it to mash the potatoes.*

═ CHICKEN UNDER A BRICK ═

SERVES 4   PREPARATION TIME: 5 MINUTES
MARINADING TIME: 2–24 HOURS   COOKING TIME: 2 HOURS

This may seem a bit weird, but weighing down the chicken like this while it cooks really packs in the flavour resulting in a roast that is juicy, tender and extra meaty. It is possible to spatchcock your chicken at home with a sharp pair of kitchen scissors – but just get your butcher to do it for you!

1 whole chicken, spatchcocked
  (get your butcher to do it)
5 tablespoons olive oil
5 sprigs of fresh rosemary

juice of 2 lemons
4 garlic cloves, peeled and crushed
salt and freshly ground black pepper

You will also need a clean house brick

Put the whole spatchcocked chicken in a dish and drizzle the oil all over the top. Work it into the skin with your hands, then season the chicken heavily with plenty of salt and pepper.

Pick off the leaves from some of the rosemary sprigs and scatter them over the chicken, then throw in the whole sprigs. Squeeze over the lemon juice and rub the crushed garlic into the skin. Leave the chicken to marinade in the fridge for anything from 2 to 24 hours, depending on how much time you have.

When you're ready to cook the chicken, preheat the oven to 180°C and heat a large frying pan or griddle pan on a medium to high heat. Place the chicken skin-side down in the pan and leave it for 4–5 minutes so it takes on a nice golden brown colour.

Place the chicken skin-side up, in a smallish roasting tray – it needs to fit quite tightly. Get a clean house brick and wrap it in several layers of foil. Push the chicken together in the tray and place the wrapped brick on top. The breast and legs should be covered, but the wings will probably be poking out the sides.

Cook the chicken in the oven for 1¼ – 1½ hours. Check it's cooked by cutting into it with a sharp knife: the juices should be clear and there shouldn't be any pink meat. Remove the brick and leave the chicken to rest in its tin for 15 minutes.

When you're ready to serve, cut the chicken into 4 pieces and serve with roast potatoes (see page 196) or a simple green salad. There's no need to make a separate gravy – just pour over the lovely cooking juices from the pan.

SAUTÉED CHICKEN LIVERS
with Marsala, grapes and shallots on toast

SERVES 4   PREPARATION TIME: 5 MINUTES   COOKING TIME: UNDER 10 MINUTES

There are lots of reasons why liver is such a classic retro ingredient: it's cheap, very nutritious and takes just a couple of minutes to cook. It can also stand up to some strong flavours, so here I've teamed it up with a splash of Marsala to produce a lovely sticky sauce. The grapes give a burst of sweet freshness.

1 tablespoon vegetable oil
1 shallot, peeled and finely diced
600g chicken livers, cleaned and trimmed
  of any white bits or sinew
4 thick slices of sourdough bread
3 tablespoons Marsala or cooking sherry

150ml double cream
100g pine nuts
150g white seedless grapes, halved
50g spinach leaves
a handful of watercress, to serve
salt and pepper

Heat the oil in a large frying pan over a medium to high heat and, when hot, fry the shallot for about 3 minutes, until softened and starting to take on colour.

Add the chicken livers, season with salt and pepper, and cook for 1½–2 minutes, stirring gently, until coloured on all sides.

While the liver is cooking, toast the sourdough slices under a hot grill or in your toaster.

Pour the sherry into the pan with the liver and let the alcohol bubble off. Gently stir in the cream, pine nuts, grapes and spinach. Bring to the boil, then remove from the heat. Season with a little more salt and pepper and serve immediately on the toasted slices of sourdough, topped with a handful of watercress.

HOME-MADE CORNED BEEF

SERVES 4   PREPARATION TIME: 30 MINUTES   BRINING TIME: 3 DAYS
CHILLING TIME: OVERNIGHT   COOKING TIME: 3 HOURS

This is quite a time investment as you need to start several days before you want to eat it, but it's worth doing as it tastes amazing! The pig's trotter releases its natural gelatine, which is what helps make it set. Some supermarkets sell pig's trotters now, but you can easily pick them up from your local butcher for next to nothing.

1.25kg beef flank
60g salt

1 pig's trotter or 15g gelatine leaves
salt and pepper

Leaving the beef in one piece, trim away the fat. Mix together 1 litre of cold water and the salt in a large bowl and submerge the beef in the brine. Leave it in the fridge for 3 days.

Remove the meat from the brine and rinse it well in fresh water. Throw away the brine.

Put the beef and the pig's trotter, if using, in a large saucepan and cover with cold water. Bring to the boil, then reduce the heat and simmer for 2–3 hours, until it is very soft. Check on it every so often and skim off any scum that rises to the surface. Remove the meat and set aside.

Strain the cooking liquid through a sieve into a clean saucepan. Heat over a medium heat for 20–30 minutes, until it has thickened and reduced by about half. This will give it a lovely rich flavour.

If you're not using the pig's trotter, soak the gelatine leaves in water until soft. Squeeze out the excess water and pour the thickened cooking liquid over the top. Stir to combine.

Finely chop the beef and place in a bowl. Pour over 300ml of the jelly liquid and mix together to coat. Taste and add a little salt and pepper if you think it needs it. Pack it into a terrine or mould and leave to set in the fridge overnight.

CORNED BEEF HASH CAKES
with fried eggs

SERVES 4   PREPARATION TIME: 20 MINUTES   COOKING TIME: 25 MINUTES

My nan loves corned beef, so this one is for her! Her classic recipe uses corned beef from a tin, which you *can* use here as well, but it will taste a whole lot better if you have the time to make your own – see the recipe opposite.

500g corned beef, chopped into 1cm dice
4 tablespoons Worcestershire sauce
2 teaspoons wholegrain mustard
700g Desiree or King Edward potatoes, unpeeled, chopped into 1cm dice
vegetable oil, for frying

2 onions, peeled and diced
2 tablespoons chopped fresh parsley
a little flour, for dusting
4 eggs
salt and pepper

Gently combine the corned beef, Worcestershire sauce and mustard in a bowl.

Boil the diced potato in a pan of salted water for about 5 minutes, until just tender. Drain in a colander, then wrap in a clean tea towel so that the cubes dry off.

Heat 1 tablespoon of oil in a frying pan and fry the onion for 2–3 minutes, until softened but not coloured.

Add the cooked potato and onion to the beef mixture along with the parsley. Mix thoroughly and season, to taste, with salt and pepper.

Using your hands, divide the mixture into four and shape into patties, each about 1.5cm thick. Dust lightly with flour.

Preheat the oven to 180°C. Wipe clean the frying pan you used for the onion and heat 2 tablespoons of oil over a medium heat. Fry the hash cakes for 2–3 minutes on each side, until they are a lovely golden brown colour. Transfer to a baking tray in the oven while you fry the eggs in a clean frying pan.

Place the cakes on warmed plates and top each one with a fried egg. Serve with plenty of brown sauce.

SPAGHETTI BOLOGNESE
with a Parmesan-herb topping

SERVES 4   PREPARATION TIME: 15 MINUTES   COOKING TIME: 4½ HOURS

Here I've taken a classic recipe and given it a touch of class. Although this takes a few hours in the oven, it really is worth it, as you'll end up with a rich, sweet, sticky ragù that will make it hard to ever go back to mince.

2 tablespoons vegetable oil
2 onions, peeled and diced
2 garlic cloves, peeled and crushed
3 or 4 sprigs of fresh thyme
1 bay leaf
2 tablespoons tomato purée
500g beef shin or stewing steak, diced
500ml beef stock
2 carrots, peeled and diced
400g tin of plum tomatoes
125ml red wine

350g spaghetti
25g butter
optional: 50ml port or Madeira
a squeeze of lemon juice, to serve
salt and pepper

for the Parmesan-herb topping
100g fresh breadcrumbs
50g finely chopped fresh herbs (a mixture
   of tarragon, parsley and chives)
50g freshly grated Parmesan cheese

Preheat the oven to 150°C. Heat the oil in a large casserole dish over a medium heat. Add the onion, garlic, thyme, bay leaf, tomato purée and the beef. Cook for 5 minutes, stirring to brown the meat on all sides. Season with salt and pepper.

Add the carrot, tomatoes and wine and bring to the boil. Simmer for a couple of minutes, then add the stock (heated so it is good and hot). Cover with the lid and transfer to the oven for about 4 hours. After a couple of hours, give everything a good stir and season with a little more salt and pepper.

Meanwhile, make the Parmesan-herb topping by mixing together all the ingredients in a small bowl. Spread the mixture on a tray and leave to dry out while the ragù cooks.

Towards the end of the cooking time, bring a large pan of salted water to the boil and cook the spaghetti according to the packet instructions.

Remove the casserole from the oven. The liquid should have reduced, leaving you with a delicious rich and sticky ragù. Stir through the butter and the port, if using.

Serve the drained spaghetti with the ragù on top and mix gently to coat the pasta. Squeeze over a little lemon juice and sprinkle with the Parmesan-herb topping.

RUMP STEAK SUPPER

with a mustard and peppercorn crust and instant tomato relish

SERVES 4 PREPARATION TIME: 10 MINUTES COOKING TIME: 40 MINUTES

Take your regular steak supper to a new level by serving it with home-made relish and chips. As well as looking pretty special, the colourful mix of peppercorns will give your steak a load of warm and fiery flavours. You can leave out the seeds of the chilli in the relish if you don't want it too hot.

4 x 225g rump steaks
4 teaspoons mixed peppercorns
  (white, black and pink)
1 tablespoon vegetable oil
4 teaspoons Dijon mustard
1 x quantity of triple-cooked chips,
  to serve (see page 198)
salt and pepper

for the relish
1 tablespoon vegetable oil
1 red onion, peeled and finely chopped
4 tomatoes, chopped
100g brown sugar
75ml red wine vinegar
½ fresh red chilli (seeds in), chopped
salt and pepper

First make the instant tomato relish. Heat the oil in a small saucepan over a medium to high heat and cook the onion for 4–5 minutes until it has just started to colour and caramelize. Season with salt and pepper, then add the tomato and stir in the sugar, vinegar and chilli. Bring to the boil, stirring occasionally, then cover and cook for 15–20 minutes. The tomatoes will be pulpy and very soft. Remove from the heat and leave to cool a little while you get on with the steaks.

Bring the steaks to room temperature. Meanwhile, dry-fry the peppercorns in a small pan for 5 minutes, then grind them to a rough powder with a pestle and mortar.

Brush the steaks all over with the oil and season with a little salt and pepper.

Preheat a griddle pan over a medium to high heat. When hot, cook the steaks for 2–3 minutes on each side for medium rare (leave them for a little longer if you like your steak more well done). Remove from the griddle and leave to rest for 2 minutes.

Brush the steaks with the mustard and scatter over the crushed peppercorns. Serve with plenty of hot chips and the relish on the side.

'When I am not cooking, Chinese food is my favourite food to eat.'

SPICY BEEF NOODLE POT

SERVES 4 **PREPARATION TIME: 15 MINUTES** **COOKING TIME: 15 MINUTES**

This may seem like a lot of ingredients to make something that you can pick up for next to nothing at your local shop, but most of them are things that will last for a long time. Once you've stocked up your cupboard, you'll be able to make one of these quicker than nipping round the corner! And it will taste so much better, of course. Get everything ready, chopped and lined up next to your pan before you start.

1 litre beef stock

4 tablespoons groundnut oil

1 teaspoon Szechuan peppercorns

1 teaspoon fennel seeds

2 tablespoons finely chopped garlic

2 tablespoons finely shredded fresh
  root ginger

2 tablespoons hot bean paste

250g steak, trimmed of fat and cut
  into thin strips

¼ teaspoon salt

¼ teaspoon caster sugar

2 tablespoons light soy sauce

1 tablespoon rice wine

150g fresh egg noodles

100g Chinese cabbage, cut into 2cm dice

4 shiitake mushrooms, stalks removed
  and sliced

1 red pepper, cut into thin strips

150g carrot, peeled and cut into thin strips

1 spring onion, trimmed and finely sliced,
  to serve

optional: 1 fresh red chilli, finely sliced,
  to serve

Get your stock nice and hot so it is ready to use. Heat a large wok over a medium to high heat. Pour in the oil and when it starts to smoke a little, stir-fry the peppercorns and fennel seeds for 30 seconds. Add the garlic, ginger and bean paste and continue to stir-fry for a couple of minutes. It should be smelling pretty tasty right now.

Add the beef strips and fry for 1 minute, then pour in the stock and add the salt, sugar, soy sauce and rice wine. Bring to the boil, then reduce to a simmer and cook for a further 10 minutes. Drop in the fresh noodles, cabbage, mushrooms, red pepper and carrot, bring back to the boil and heat through for 2 minutes.

Divide into four bowls and serve sprinkled with the sliced spring onion and the chilli, if you like it extra spicy.

ROASTED COD IN PARSLEY SAUCE

SERVES 4   PREPARATION TIME: 15 MINUTES   COOKING TIME: 20 MINUTES

Boil-in-the-bag cod with peas, potatoes and parsley sauce was a regular dinner round our house. Here's my version of that classic from when I was growing up. Always try to source sustainable fish where you can. Good alternatives to cod are haddock, coley and pollock – they all have firm, white flesh that can stand up to cooking in the oven without drying out. My parsley sauce has chervil added for extra flavour and I've blitzed it so it's an amazing green colour!

1 tablespoon vegetable oil
4 x 175g cod steaks (skin on)
juice of ½ lemon
1 x quantity of pan-fried Jersey Royals, to serve (see page 202)
salt and pepper

for the parsley sauce
1 shallot, peeled and finely chopped
5 white peppercorns
1 tablespoon vegetable oil
120ml white wine
250ml double cream
30g fresh flat-leaf parsley leaves
20g fresh chervil leaves
juice of ½ lemon
salt and pepper

Preheat the oven to 200°C. Heat the oil in a large frying pan over a medium heat. Season the fish with salt and pepper, then place it in the hot pan and cook for 2 minutes, until just starting to colour.

Transfer the fish to a baking dish and cook in the oven for 10–15 minutes, until just cooked and opaque all the way through (the length of time this will take will depend on the thickness of the fish).

Meanwhile, make the sauce by sweating the shallot and peppercorns in oil over a medium to high heat. Add the wine and leave to reduce by half. Stir through the cream and leave to bubble and simmer for about 5 minutes, until it starts to thicken.

While the sauce is cooking, boil the kettle. Place the herbs in a small bowl, then pour hot water over the top, just to cover them, and leave for 2 minutes. This will help them keep their lovely bright colour when they are added to the sauce. Drain and set aside.

Tip the creamy sauce into a blender. Season with the lemon juice and some salt and pepper. Add the drained herbs and blitz until you have a vibrant green, smooth sauce.

Remove the fish from the oven, squeeze over the lemon juice and serve with the sauce and Jersey Royals.

SMOKED HADDOCK AND CRAB CAKES

SERVES 4   PREPARATION TIME: 10 MINUTES   COOKING TIME: 40 MINUTES

Haddock and crab give these fishcakes a brilliant creamy texture and, unlike the ones you can buy in the supermarkets, they are more fish than potato! Serve with loads of the tartare sauce and a crunchy green salad. You can also freeze these and cook them straight from frozen – they will take a bit longer in the oven – and check they are hot all the way through before serving.

200g Desiree potatoes, peeled and halved

200g white crabmeat

200g smoked undyed haddock fillet,
  skin removed

1 tablespoon chopped fresh dill

1 tablespoon chopped fresh coriander

2 tablespoons chopped fresh parsley

1 tablespoon Dijon mustard

100g plain flour

2 eggs, whisked with a splash of water

120g fresh breadcrumbs

1 tablespoon vegetable oil, for frying

salt and pepper

for the tartare sauce

220g mayonnaise

1 tablespoon chopped green olives

1 tablespoon chopped capers

1 tablespoon chopped gherkins

1 tablespoon chopped fresh parsley

1 tablespoon chopped fresh tarragon

juice and zest of 1 lemon

First, make the mash. Bring a large pan of salted water to the boil and cook the potatoes for 15–20 minutes, until tender. Drain, then mash until smooth. Don't use any butter or milk, as you want the mash to be quite dry. Leave to cool a little.

While the potatoes are cooking, make the tartare sauce by combining all the ingredients in a small bowl. Chill in the fridge.

When the potato is cool enough to handle, mix it together with the crab, fish, herbs and mustard and season with plenty of salt and pepper.

Preheat the oven to 180°C. Divide the potato mixture into 6 equal portions and shape into fat fishcakes.

Tip the flour into a shallow bowl, the egg into another bowl and the breadcrumbs into a third. Dip the fishcakes first in the flour, shaking off the excess, then dip them in the egg and finally into the breadcrumbs, making sure they are fully coated and the crumbs are pressed firmly into the fishcakes.

Heat the oil in a large frying pan over a medium heat and cook the fishcakes for 2–3 minutes on each side until golden brown. Transfer to a baking tray and cook in the oven for 15 minutes. Serve with plenty of tartare sauce.

FISH SUPPER

SERVES 4   PREPARATION TIME: 15 MINUTES   COOKING TIME: 10–15 MINUTES

A fish supper on a Friday night at home was a real treat and something we all looked forward to. Here, I've combined the two fish and chip essentials, peas and tartare sauce, into a delicious side. Serve with loads of hot chips to dip. Coley and pollock are good choices here if you can't get yourself some sustainable cod.

vegetable oil, for frying

4 x 150g firm white fish fillets (skin on)

100g plain flour, seasoned with salt and pepper

1 x quantity of triple-cooked chips, to serve (see page 198)

for the beer batter

250ml lager

150–200g plain flour, plus extra for dusting

salt and pepper

for the tartare peas

300g frozen peas

3 tablespoons crème fraîche

1 tablespoon chopped green olives

1 tablespoon chopped fresh dill

1 tablespoon chopped capers

juice and zest of ½ lemon

Bring a pan of salted water to the boil and cook the peas for 5 minutes. Drain well and then stir through the rest of the ingredients for the tartare peas. Set aside while you cook the fish.

In a large bowl, mix together the beer and 150g flour and season with salt and pepper. The batter should have a fairly thick consistency and coat the back of the spoon. Add the rest of the flour if it seems a little thin.

Heat the oil in a deep-fat fryer to 190°C or pour oil into a heavy-bottomed pan to a depth of about 10cm and heat over a medium heat until a little cube of bread dropped into the oil fizzes and turns brown in about 30 seconds.

Dust the fillets in the seasoned flour, shaking off the excess. Dip them into the batter and then straight into the hot oil. Cook for about 4 minutes, until crispy and golden brown. (You may need to cook these in batches so you don't overcrowd your fryer. Keep them warm in a low oven while you cook the rest.) Drain on some kitchen roll, then serve with chips and a generous pile of tartare peas. To add a nice finishing touch, scatter some dill over the dish once cooked – it works so well with fish.

SMOKED HADDOCK SCOTCH EGG
with curry mayonnaise

SERVES 4   PREPARATION TIME: 25 MINUTES   CHILLING TIME: 45 MINUTES
COOKING TIME: 25–35 MINUTES

Any firm white fish will work well in these Scotch eggs, making a lovely contrast to the smoky haddock, but I think plaice and lemon sole are my favourites.

for the curry mayonnaise
1 tablespoon olive oil
½ onion, peeled and finely diced
1 tablespoon mild curry powder
½ teaspoon mustard powder
175ml mayonnaise
2 tablespoons double cream
1 tablespoon mango chutney
juice of ½ lemon
2 tablespoons chopped fresh coriander
salt

for the Scotch egg
180g smoked undyed haddock fillet, skin removed, cut into quarters

200ml milk
5 eggs at room temperature, plus 1 egg white
25g butter
1 leek, trimmed, white part only, diced
200g white fish fillet, skin removed, roughly chopped
100ml double cream
½ teaspoon paprika
2 teaspoons lemon juice
50g plain flour
75g dry breadcrumbs
1 litre vegetable oil, for deep-frying
salt and pepper

First, make the curry mayonnaise by heating the oil in a small saucepan over a medium heat. Add the onion and a pinch of salt and cook for 5 minutes, until softened. Reduce the heat to low and stir in the curry and mustard powders. Keep stirring for about a minute, so that the spices don't burn. Turn off the heat and leave to cool.

Mix the mayonnaise, cream, mango chutney and lemon juice together with the cooled onion. Chill in the fridge until needed.

Place the pieces of haddock in a small saucepan and pour over the milk so that it covers the fish. Bring to the boil, reduce the heat and gently simmer for 5 minutes. Use a slotted spoon to remove the fish from the milk and place it on some kitchen roll to drain and cool. Throw away the milk.

Fill a large pan with cold water and add four of the eggs. As soon as it boils, time 2½ minutes for soft yolks and 5 minutes for set yolks. Remove the eggs from the pan and plunge them into very cold water for a few minutes. When cool enough to handle, carefully peel them. Rinse and pat dry with kitchen roll and set aside.

Meanwhile, melt the butter in a small saucepan and cook the diced leek for 4–5 minutes, until softened but not coloured. Remove from the heat and set aside.

Place the white fish in a food processor with the egg white and season well with salt. Blitz to a smooth purée, then slowly add the cream until it is totally incorporated and you have a smooth, firm paste. The mousse must be firm and not runny – if it seems really stiff, add a touch more cream. Finally, add the paprika, a little pepper and the lemon juice.

Flake the cooled haddock into the fish mousse along with the cooked leeks. Mix gently but thoroughly to combine. Divide the mousse into quarters and place one portion on a square of clingfilm approx. 25cm x 25cm. Flatten it out to form a round about 1cm thick. Place a peeled egg in the middle, then draw up the four corners of the cling film, pushing the mousse against the egg and squashing out any air as you go. Once the mousse is sealed around the egg, twist the corners of the clingfilm together at the top of the egg. Repeat with the remaining mousse and eggs and then place on a plate (still in the clingfilm) and chill in the fridge for at least 30 minutes to firm up.

When you're ready to cook your eggs, peel off the clingfilm. Use your hands to smooth the mousse coating and create a good round shape. Place the flour in a shallow bowl, the remaining egg in a second one and the breadcrumbs in a third. Roll each egg first in the flour, then in the beaten egg and finally in the breadcrumbs, making sure they are fully coated. Return them to the fridge to rest for a further 10 minutes.

Heat the oil in a deep-fat fryer to 180°C (or pour the oil into a large deep pan set over a medium heat). Cook the eggs, one at a time, depending on the size of your fryer or pan (it's important not to overcrowd the fryer or pan as the temperature of the oil will drop, resulting in soggy breadcrumbs). Fry for 3–4 minutes, or until golden brown, then carefully remove from the oil, drain on some kitchen roll and season with salt.

Leave to cool slightly before serving with a generous dollop of curry mayonnaise topped with coriander.

SARDINES AND TOAST
with cherry tomato salsa

SERVES 4   PREPARATION TIME: 5 MINUTES   COOKING TIME: 5–10 MINUTES

Fresh sardines are great as a quick meal – and they're cheap and healthy too. Rather than serve them on slices of toast, I've made a flavoured breadcrumb mix to scatter over the fish. The crumbs will soak up all the lovely juices.

12 fresh sardines, filleted
2 tablespoons extra virgin olive oil
2 sprigs of fresh rosemary
lemon wedges, to serve
salt and pepper

for the breadcrumbs
3 tablespoons butter
200g fresh breadcrumbs
1 tablespoon chopped fresh parsley

1 tablespoon capers
salt and pepper

for the cherry tomato salsa
300g cherry tomatoes, halved
24 black olives, pitted and diced
12 fresh basil leaves, roughly chopped
1 fresh red chilli, deseeded and sliced
2 tablespoons extra virgin olive oil

First make the salsa by mixing together all the ingredients in a small bowl. Leave to one side for the flavours to combine while you cook the sardines.

Preheat the grill to high. Cut the sardines almost through horizontally and open out like a book. Arrange the butterflied sardines skin side up in a roasting tin. Drizzle over the olive oil and nestle in the rosemary sprigs. Season with salt and pepper, then grill for 4–5 minutes, until cooked through.

Meanwhile, heat the butter in a frying pan over a medium heat until it starts to foam. Stir in the breadcrumbs and cook, stirring almost constantly, for 5–10 minutes, so that the breadcrumbs absorb the butter and they start to brown and crisp up. Mix through the parsley and capers. Season with salt and pepper.

Scatter some toasted breadcrumbs on to each serving plate and top with 3 sardines. Sprinkle more crumbs on the top. Spoon the salsa on the side and serve with lemon wedges to squeeze over the top.

SAUSAGE ROLLS
with cracked pink peppercorn sauce

MAKES 15   PREPARATION TIME: 20 MINUTES   COOKING TIME: 30 MINUTES

This is my favourite kind of eating! Serve a big pile of sausage rolls in the middle of the table with a jug of the pink peppercorn sauce and a bowl of cabbage and bacon with celeriac and carrot (see page 187). And let everyone dig in.

400g sausage meat
1 onion, peeled and finely diced
½ teaspoon chopped fresh thyme
½ teaspoon chopped fresh parsley
½ teaspoon chopped fresh sage
zest of 1 lemon
1 teaspoon salt
1 teaspoon black pepper
a little plain flour, for dusting
200g puff pastry
1 egg, whisked with 2 teaspoons milk

for the cracked pink peppercorn sauce
1 tablespoon olive oil
1 shallot, peeled and finely chopped
3 garlic cloves, peeled and crushed
4 tablespoons pink peppercorns
50ml brandy
200ml beef stock
200ml double cream
2 tablespoons chopped fresh tarragon
salt and pepper

Preheat the oven to 200°C. Mix the sausage meat in a bowl with the onion, chopped herbs, lemon zest, salt and pepper. Set aside and chill in the fridge.

Roll out the pastry on a lightly floured surface into a rectangle with a thickness of just under 5mm. Cut the pastry into 3 strips, each roughly 15cm wide. Mould the sausage meat mixture into 3 sausage shapes the same length as the pastry and sit each one, off-centre, on top of a strip of pastry. Brush the other side of the pastry with the egg mixture, then roll over from the sausage side to seal.

Once rolled, cut each pastry-wrapped sausage into 5 pieces and place on a baking sheet. Cut a small hole with a knife in the top of each sausage roll (to let the steam escape as it cooks) and brush with more egg. Bake for 30 minutes until golden brown. Leave to cool a little before serving.

For the sauce, heat the oil in a frying pan over a medium heat and cook the shallot and garlic with the peppercorns for about 5 minutes. The onion should be nice and soft. Add the brandy and let it reduce by about half. Season with salt and pepper and pour in the stock. Reduce the heat and simmer for about 3 minutes, then stir through the cream. Simmer gently for about 10–15 minutes, until it's lovely and thick. Just before serving, stir through the tarragon. Transfer to a jug or bowl and serve with the sausage rolls.

GAMMON, EGG AND PINEAPPLE SALSA

SERVES 4   PREPARATION TIME: 15 MINUTES   COOKING TIME: 10 MINUTES

A real classic tea from my childhood that my mum used to cook for me. I've given it a bit of a twist with a pineapple and chilli salsa, rather than one of those syrupy pineapple rings from a tin. It's much better for cutting through the sweet flavour of the gammon too.

4 x 170g gammon steaks
6 tablespoons maple syrup
1 tablespoon vegetable oil
4 eggs

for the pineapple salsa
1 teaspoon mustard seeds
½ juicy fresh pineapple, peeled and diced (approx. 300g)
1 tablespoon roughly chopped fresh coriander leaves
1 fresh red chilli, deseeded and finely sliced
zest and juice of 1 lime

First make the salsa. Dry-fry the mustard seeds for 30 seconds–1 minute, until just starting to brown. Tip them into a bowl and mix together with the rest of the salsa ingredients, making sure to incorporate all the juice from the pineapple.

Preheat the grill to high. Place the gammon steaks on a grill rack with a tray underneath. Cook the steaks for 8–10 minutes, basting with maple syrup every minute and turning them over halfway through. They should be sticky, richly coloured and cooked through.

Meanwhile, heat the oil in a frying pan and fry the eggs for 4 minutes (or until cooked to your liking).

Serve each gammon steak drizzled with a little of the juices from the grill pan, with an egg on top and the zingy salsa on the side.

PAN-FRIED PORK CHOPS
with black pudding croquettes and cider and apple sauce

SERVES 4   PREPARATION TIME: 15 MINUTES   CHILLING TIME: 30 MINUTES
COOKING TIME: 35 MINUTES

Pork, apple and black pudding are a winning combination. Here, the black pudding is in the fluffy potato croquettes, which you can use to soak up all the sticky cider sauce from the pan.

1 tablespoon vegetable oil
4 x 225g pork chops
a few sprigs of fresh thyme

for the black pudding croquettes
1kg Desiree or Maris Piper potatoes, peeled and halved
2 tablespoons butter
1 heaped tablespoon wholegrain mustard
2 tablespoons finely chopped fresh chives
150ml double cream
150g black pudding, crumbled

for the sauce
2 apples, cored and cut into eighths
200ml cider
200ml single cream
1 teaspoon mustard
1 teaspoon finely chopped fresh tarragon leaves
salt and pepper

First make the croquettes by following the recipe on page 199 until you reach the stage when you have mashed the potatoes with the butter, mustard, chives and cream. At this point, gently mix in the crumbled black pudding. Continue following the remainder of the recipe. When you put the croquettes in the oven, make a start on the chops.

Heat the oil in a frying pan over a medium to high heat. When hot, add the chops and the thyme sprigs. Cook the chops for 4 minutes on each side, then transfer to a plate and cover in foil to keep them warm. Remove the thyme from the pan.

With the pan still over the heat, add the pieces of apple. Stir them around so that they absorb the juices from cooking the pork and pick up any sticky bits on the bottom of the pan. Pour in the cider and leave it to bubble away until it has reduced by about half. Stir in the cream and cook for about 5 minutes, until slightly thickened. Finish the sauce by stirring through the mustard and tarragon. Season, to taste, with salt and pepper.

Serve the well-rested chops with the sauce and the croquettes on the side.

BREADED LAMB CUTLETS
stuffed with goat's cheese

SERVES 4   PREPARATION TIME: 15 MINUTES   COOKING TIME: 30 MINUTES

These look very impressive, but they're actually incredibly easy to make – perfect for a midweek dinner. You can make life even easier for yourself by using bought breadcrumbs (you will need 200g) or making some ahead of time and keeping them in an airtight container. Look for plump lamb cutlets or a rack of lamb, separating the cutlets out yourself.

8 lamb cutlets
80g soft goat's cheese
60g plain flour
1 large egg, beaten
180g butter
2 tablespoons olive oil
lemon wedges, to serve

for the breadcrumbs
200g ciabatta bread
1 tablespoon fresh rosemary
  leaves, chopped
1 teaspoon chilli flakes
1 tablespoon sea salt
3 tablespoons olive oil
pepper

First make the breadcrumbs by preheating the oven to 180°C. Tear the ciabatta bread into small chunks and arrange on a baking tray. Sprinkle over the chopped rosemary and chilli flakes and season with the sea salt. Drizzle with olive oil and mix together with your hands, then cook in the oven for 5–8 minutes, until they are crunchy and a rich golden colour. Remove from the oven and allow to cool before tipping into a food processor. Pulse to form coarse – not fine – breadcrumbs, then season with pepper, tip into a shallow bowl and set aside.

Create a pocket in each lamb cutlet by holding the bone edge of the cutlet firmly on a board and inserting the point of the knife slowly into the opposite edge, piercing horizontally into the meat towards the bone to create a 1cm slit. Stuff each pocket with a small amount of goat's cheese (about the size of a marble), pressing down on the meat to seal the cheese inside.

Turn up the oven temperature to 200°C. Tip the flour into a shallow bowl and the beaten egg into another. Dip each cutlet first in the flour, shaking to remove the excess, then in the egg and finish by coating in the breadcrumbs, using your hands to press the crumbs into the meat.

Place the breaded cutlets in a baking dish, drizzle with olive oil and cook for 20 minutes. Serve with lemon wedges to squeeze over the top. They are very good served with pan-fried Jersey Royals (see page 202).

 SHEPHERD'S PIE

SERVES 4   PREPARATION TIME: 10 MINUTES   COOKING TIME: 1½ HOURS

You can't beat a good old-fashioned shepherd's pie. In my version, I've grated the veggies so that they cook quickly with the mince. This will make them nice and soft and you'll also get much more flavour out of them.

1 tablespoon vegetable oil
1 large white onion, peeled and grated
2 garlic cloves, peeled and grated
100g diced bacon or pancetta
a few sprigs of fresh thyme, leaves picked
500g lamb mince
2 carrots, peeled and grated
150ml red wine
2 tablespoons Worcestershire sauce

2 tablespoons HP brown sauce
550ml chicken stock
salt and pepper

for the parsnip and potato mash
300g potatoes, peeled and halved
200g parsnips, peeled and chopped
  into chunks
150ml milk
50g butter

Heat the oil in a large saucepan over a medium heat and fry the onion, garlic, bacon and thyme for 4–5 minutes, until the onion is nice and soft and the bacon has started to colour and release its lovely flavour.

Add the lamb and cook for 5 minutes, stirring often, until it is brown all over. Stir in the grated carrot and the wine. Bring the wine to the boil and cook until it has reduced by about a third. Add the Worcestershire sauce and brown sauce and cover with the stock. Bring to the boil again, then reduce the heat and simmer for 45 minutes–1 hour, until the liquid has thickened – it should be the consistency of thick gravy. If it's still very liquidy, turn up the heat and let it bubble away rapidly for a couple of minutes. Season, to taste, but you shouldn't really need any salt as the bacon will have got that covered.

While the mince is cooking, make the mash. Bring a large pan of salted water to the boil and cook the potatoes and parsnips for 15–20 minutes, until tender. Place the milk and butter in a small pan and heat over a medium heat until the butter has completely melted. Drain the cooked veg, return to the hot pan and mash with the milk and butter until smooth. Preheat the oven to 180°C.

Spread the mince mixture evenly in a baking dish and smooth the mash over the top. Cook for 30 minutes, until golden brown and bubbling away around the sides. Serve with red cabbage (see page 191).

MAC 'N' CHEESE

A plate of creamy, oozy macaroni cheese is one of the most comforting dishes around. I like to add bacon to mine, but you can leave it out if you'd like to keep it vegetarian. You can also replace the asparagus with any green veg you like – chopped green beans work well.

400g macaroni
2 tablespoons pine nuts
½ tablespoon olive oil
optional: 150g bacon pieces or
  cubes of pancetta
1 teaspoon fresh thyme leaves

12 asparagus spears, woody ends
  removed and chopped into 2cm pieces
100g mascarpone cheese
120g Cheddar cheese, grated
salt and pepper

Preheat the oven to 170°C. Cook the macaroni in a large pan of salted water according to the packet instructions. When cooked, remove 250ml of the cooking water with a ladle and pour it into a jug. Drain the pasta, return it to the pan and set aside.

While the macaroni is cooking, heat a medium frying pan over a medium heat and add the pine nuts. Turn down the heat to low and toast the pine nuts gently until golden. Tip them into a bowl and return the pan to the heat.

Add the oil to the pan and fry the bacon (if using) for 2–3 minutes until just cooked. If you're not using bacon, just heat the oil in the pan. Remove the pan containing the cooked bacon or just the oil from the heat, then add the thyme leaves and asparagus pieces and toss to coat in the oil. Season with a little salt (if using the bacon, salt may be unnecessary).

Add to the pan containing the cooked macaroni and stir in the mascarpone, 100g of the Cheddar and the toasted pine nuts. Turn on the heat to low, add a glug of the reserved cooking water, mix to combine and keep adding the water, a little at a time, to create a creamy, cheesy sauce. You may not need all the water, but the sauce needs to be quite runny as the pasta will continue to soak it up as it cooks in the oven.

Tip the mixture into an ovenproof dish, cover with foil and bake in the oven for 10 minutes. Remove the foil and top with the remaining Cheddar and a twist of black pepper. Finish the mac and cheese under a hot grill for a couple of minutes so that the cheese bubbles and browns. Serve with a green salad or a mound of pea shoots.

BEANS ON TOAST

SERVES 4   PREPARATION TIME: 20 MINUTES   COOKING TIME: 15 MINUTES

Last year, nearly 900 million tins of Heinz baked beans were eaten in the UK, according to their website. For when you fancy something a bit different, try this tasty little number. The ricotta, mint and lemon juice bring it to life and give it a fresh zingy taste and the salad adds a great texture. Delicious.

150g podded broad beans
4 thick slices of sourdough bread
1 tablespoon olive oil
2 garlic cloves, peeled and crushed
200g peas
8 tablespoons ricotta
1 tablespoon chopped fresh mint

juice of ½ lemon
salt and pepper

for the salad
50g lamb's lettuce
25g Parmesan cheese, grated
1½ tablespoons olive oil

Bring a saucepan of salted water to the boil and blanch the broad beans for 3 minutes. Drain and cool under cold running water. Slip the beans out of their outer skins, tip into a bowl and set aside.

To make the salad, combine all the ingredients in a bowl and toss together to coat evenly. Season to taste.

Heat a griddle pan over a high heat. Place the slices of sourdough on a baking tray or plate and drizzle with the oil. Spread the crushed garlic evenly over one side of each piece of bread and transfer to the hot griddle. Cook for 2–3 minutes on each side, until lightly browned and slightly toasted.

Meanwhile, bring a saucepan of water to the boil and blanch the peas for 2 minutes. Cool under cold running water, then add to the bowl with the broad beans.

Mix the beans and peas with the ricotta, mint and lemon juice and season, to taste, with salt and pepper. Spoon over the hot toast (garlic side up) and serve with the salad.

PEA AND GOAT'S CHEESE RISOTTO

SERVES 4   PREPARATION TIME: 10 MINUTES   COOKING TIME: 25 MINUTES

Risotto was one of the very first things I learned to cook when I started being a chef. You can pretty much use any ingredients in a risotto, which is why they're so brilliant (I used to make one with chives, tomatoes and haddock at the first place I worked at). I've chosen a very British combination of flavours here, and the goat's cheese will make it deliciously creamy.

1 tablespoon butter
2 garlic cloves, peeled and crushed
1 shallot, peeled and finely diced
200g Arborio rice
150ml white wine
500ml hot vegetable stock

200g fresh or frozen peas
100g goat's cheese
juice of ½ lemon
125g pea shoots
1 tablespoon olive oil
salt and pepper

Heat the butter in a large saucepan until it starts to foam. Add the garlic and shallot and cook for 3 minutes. Season with salt and pepper. Stir in the rice, making sure it is coated in all the sweet buttery onions, then pour in the wine and keep stirring until it has bubbled away.

Add the hot stock in three batches, stirring continuously between each addition until it has been completely absorbed. This should take about 15 minutes. The rice should be cooked through, but still a little firm to the bite.

To finish the risotto, remove the pan from the heat and stir through the peas, cheese and lemon juice. Season, to taste, with salt and pepper, then give it one more stir and plate up. Dress the pea shoots with the oil and a little salt and scatter over the top of the risotto.

RETRO *Feasts*

This chapter is all about celebrating, and what better way to do that than through sharing a meal with friends and family.

Having people over for dinner doesn't have to mean formal dining and three courses and a coffee. A big pot of curry in the middle of the table, so everyone can help themselves, or a pie straight from the oven, and you have yourself a brilliant meal that everyone will love, without any of the palaver.

A lot of these recipes are a bit of an adventurous take on very traditional British dishes – it's all about having some fun with food and playing around with what you already know. Try my version of duck à l'orange made with orange cordial – it's sticky and sweet and ridiculously moreish. Or maybe a luxury fish pie? Whatever you go for, pour yourself a drink and cook up a retro feast to remember!

* CHICKEN KIEV *

* CHICKEN CURRY WITH RICE AND SUGAR SNAP PEAS *

* DUCK LEGS WITH AN ORANGE CORDIAL GLAZE *

* TRAY-BAKED PASTA AND MEATBALLS *

* STEAK AND KIDNEY PIE *

* FILLET OF BEEF 'WELLY' *

* SPICED ROAST LEG OF LAMB WITH TZATZIKI *

* LAMB HOTPOT *

* SWEET-AND-SOUR PORK BROTH
WITH PINEAPPLE AND BOK CHOY *

* SAUSAGE STEW *

* PIG IN A BUN *

* FISH PIE *

* SURF AND TURF: GRILLED VEAL CHOPS,
TUNA AND CAPER SAUCE *

* GRILLED SALMON WITH LETTUCE,
CUCUMBER AND TOMATO *

* GNOCCHI WITH WILD MUSHROOM RAGÙ *

* THREE CHEESE VEGETABLE LASAGNE *

CHICKEN KIEV

SERVES 4   PREPARATION TIME: 25 MINUTES   CHILLING TIME: 10 MINUTES   COOKING TIME: 20 MINUTES

How annoying was it when all the garlic filling burst out of your Kiev in the oven! Make sure you wrap up the garlic butter nice and tight so none of it escapes! For the ultimate retro dinner party, serve these with the croquettes on page 199.

100g butter, softened
4 garlic cloves, peeled and finely chopped
2 tablespoons finely chopped fresh parsley
zest and juice of 1 lemon
4 skinless chicken breasts
80g plain flour, seasoned with
  2 teaspoons paprika

2 eggs, beaten
200g white breadcrumbs
2 tablespoons oil, for frying
salt and pepper

8–16 cocktail sticks

Mix the softened butter with the garlic, parsley, lemon zest and juice and season with salt and pepper. Shape into 4 small logs, and then place in the fridge to chill for about 10 minutes.

Preheat the oven to 200°C. Lay a chicken breast flat on the work surface upside-down. Remove the small inner fillet. Using a sharp knife, make an incision into the breast to form a pocket and stuff in a butter log. Place the small fillet on top to conceal the butter. Secure with cocktail sticks and repeat with the other chicken breasts and butter logs.

Place the seasoned flour in a shallow bowl, the egg in a second bowl and the bread-crumbs in a third. Dip each chicken breast first in the flour, then in the egg and finally in the breadcrumbs. Make sure the chicken is completely covered in the breadcrumbs and press them in firmly.

Heat the oil in a large frying pan and when it is hot, fry the Kievs for 4–5 minutes, turning halfway through, until golden brown and crispy all over. Transfer to a baking tray and cook in the oven for 15 minutes. Remove the cocktail sticks and serve with mashed potato or the croquettes on page 199 to soak up all the lovely garlicky juices.

CHICKEN CURRY
with rice and sugar snap peas

SERVES 4–6   PREPARATION TIME: 10 MINUTES   COOKING TIME: 30 MINUTES

A big pot of curry in the middle of the table with a pile of poppadoms and some steaming rice is my favourite kind of low-effort entertaining. The mango in this curry gives it a really fresh taste and a creamy texture – and it's much cheaper and healthier than dialling the local takeaway. The rice is inspired by my dad, who would make this for me all the time.

2 tablespoons vegetable oil

2 onions, peeled and very finely minced

2 garlic cloves, peeled and very finely minced

600g skinless chicken breasts, cut into 2cm dice

3 tablespoons curry paste (your favourite from a jar or use the recipe below)

400g tin of chopped tomatoes

2 courgettes, cut into 1cm dice

1 small fresh mango, peeled and cut into 1cm dice

1 tablespoon chopped fresh coriander

butter

coconut flakes

sugar snap peas

lime wedges, to serve

1 fresh red chilli, finely sliced, to garnish

home-made curry paste

2 teaspoons cumin seeds

3 teaspoons coriander seeds

1 teaspoon black mustard seeds

2 teaspoons ground turmeric

1 thumb-sized piece of fresh root ginger, peeled and grated

3 cloves garlic, peeled and roughly chopped

1 fresh red chilli, chopped

3 tablespoons tomato purée

To make the curry paste, in a small pan over a medium heat, dry-fry the cumin, coriander and mustard seeds for 3–4 minutes, until the mustard seeds start to pop. Remove from the heat and allow to cool a little before crushing to a powder in a pestle and mortar.

Add the turmeric, ginger, garlic and chilli and pound to a fine paste. Mix in the tomato purée to bind everything together. The curry paste will keep in an airtight container in the fridge for a few days. Preheat the oven to 180°C.

Heat the oil in a large saucepan over a medium heat. Cook the onion and garlic for 4 minutes, until softened and starting to take on a little colour. Add the chicken pieces and the curry paste. Mix to coat the onion and chicken in the curry paste and cook for about 4 minutes, until lightly browned.

Stir in the tomatoes and the courgettes. Bring to the boil and simmer for 5 minutes until the sauce has thickened. Stir through the mango pieces and the coriander.

Serve the curry with a generous mound of rice and some lime wedges to squeeze over the top. Garnish with chopped chilli and coriander leaves and top with a dollop of the cool yoghurt sauce.

Rice

To make the rice heat 2 tablespoons of oil in an ovenproof casserole dish over a medium heat. Gently fry 1 chopped onion and 2 cloves of garlic, peeled and finely chopped. Add 2 star anise, 3 cardamom pods and 1 bay leaf and cook for 5 minutes until the onion and garlic have softened and the spices have released some of their flavours. It should start to smell delicious.

Add 300g of long grain rice and stir to coat in the spices, then pour in 1 400ml tin of coconut milk and 100ml water. Cover with a lid, bring to the boil and then transfer to the preheated oven and cook for 10–15 minutes, or until the rice is tender, but with a slight bite (keep an eye on it to make sure it doesn't dry out; adding a splash more water if necessary).

Remove the rice from the oven and stir through the butter, using a fork to fluff up the rice. Gently fold through the crumbled coconut flakes and sliced sugar snap peas.

Yoghurt sauce

Just before serving, mix together 4 heaped tablespoons of natural yoghurt, a 10cm piece of cucumber, halved lengthways, seeds removed and finely diced, and 1 table-spoon of finely chopped fresh mint leaves to make the yoghurt sauce.

DUCK LEGS
with an orange cordial glaze

This is my twist on the traditional duck à l'orange. It might sound a bit unusual, but trust me, it's delicious. The sugars in the cordial make the sauce lovely and sticky. Serve with sautéed potatoes and steamed green beans for a really retro feel.

6 duck legs (skin on)
250g button onions, peeled
2 oranges, halved, juice squeezed
  and shells reserved
1 tablespoon coriander seeds

150ml orange cordial
  (e.g. Robinsons squash)
3 tablespoons balsamic vinegar
salt and pepper

To remove some of the fat from the duck legs, place them in a large pan of simmering water for about 15 minutes. Drain, then pat them dry with kitchen roll. Arrange them in a roasting tin in a single layer – they should fit quite snugly. Scatter over the button onions and season with salt and pepper.

Preheat the oven to 180°C. Chop each reserved orange shell into three wedges and place in a large bowl. Bash the coriander seeds in a pestle and mortar. Add the orange cordial, orange juice, vinegar and coriander seeds to the orange shells and mix well.

Pour the mixture over the duck legs in the roasting tin and mix to coat thoroughly. Cook in the preheated oven for about 1¼ hours. The duck will have a lovely glaze and be a little bit sticky and the onions will be very soft. Discard the orange shells and serve.

TIP: *You can use frozen onions in this recipe to save some prep time.*

TRAY-BAKED PASTA AND MEATBALLS

SERVES 6   PREPARATION TIME: 30 MINUTES   COOKING TIME: 1 HOUR 10 MINUTES

In this recipe, the pasta and meatballs are layered up with a rich tomato sauce and loads of cheese and baked in the oven. Cooking the meatballs like this keeps them really juicy. It's a brilliant, cheesy, decadent take on a very retro dinner.

300g penne or rigatoni

2 tablespoons olive oil

250g buffalo mozzarella, torn
  into small bite-sized pieces

200g Parmesan cheese, grated

6 slices of Parma ham, cut into thin strips

16 basil leaves

for the meatballs

100g minced beef

100g minced pork

80g salami (preferably mortadella), diced

80g Parmesan cheese, grated

100g fresh white breadcrumbs

2 eggs, beaten

2 tablespoons roughly chopped fresh
  flat-leaf parsley

2 tablespoons plain flour, for dusting

2 tablespoons olive oil

for the tomato sauce

100ml olive oil

1 red onion, peeled and finely diced

2 garlic cloves, peeled and finely chopped

3 x 400g tins of plum tomatoes

16 fresh basil leaves

To make the tomato sauce, heat the oil in a saucepan and gently fry, without colouring, the onion and garlic. Next, add the tinned plum tomatoes and basil, season with salt and pepper and bring to the boil. Lower the heat and simmer for 30–40 minutes, stirring occasionally to break up the tomatoes. Taste again and adjust the seasoning.

Meanwhile, make the meatballs. Combine all the ingredients except the flour and oil in a mixing bowl and season with salt and pepper. Use your hands to mix everything together. Roll the meatball mixture into small marbles, then dust with the flour. Heat the oil in a frying pan over a low to medium heat and gently fry the meatballs until lightly browned all over. Don't overcrowd the pan – you may need to do this in batches. Remove from the pan and set aside. Preheat your oven to 180°C.

Towards the end of the sauce cooking time, cook the penne in boiling salted water until al dente. Drain and toss in the olive oil to prevent it sticking. Carefully mix together the meatballs, cooked pasta and tomato sauce.

Spread about one-third of the meatballs and pasta mix over the bottom of a 25cm x 32cm ovenproof dish. Scatter over roughly one-third of the buffalo mozzarella pieces, the grated Parmesan, the Parma ham strips and the basil leaves. Continue to build the layers, finishing with a layer of buffalo mozzarella and Parmesan. Bake in the preheated oven for 30 minutes, until golden brown on top and bubbling.

≡ STEAK AND KIDNEY PIE ≡

SERVES 6   PREPARATION TIME: 20 MINUTES   COOLING TIME: 30 MINUTES   COOKING TIME: 2 HOURS

Why mess around with something so good? This is quite a traditional recipe, but I've made it extra luxurious by using field mushrooms so it's really hearty and rich. The filling can be made a day in advance – the flavours are even better the next day – perfect for dunking your pastry in!

700g chuck steak, cut into 2.5cm dice

250g lambs' kidneys, trimmed and cut into 2.5cm dice

1 tablespoon beef dripping or vegetable oil

50g butter

2 onions, peeled and cut into 1cm dice

3 carrots, peeled and cut into 1cm dice

4 flat field mushrooms, cut into thick slices

1 tablespoon tomato purée

1 bay leaf

600ml hot beef stock

2 teaspoons Worcestershire sauce

350g puff pastry

1 egg, beaten

salt and pepper

Season the steak and kidneys with plenty of salt and pepper. Heat the beef dripping or oil in a large frying pan over a medium to high heat and, when hot, add the seasoned steak. Cook for 5–10 minutes, until sealed on all sides and a rich brown colour. Transfer the meat to a large saucepan.

Still over a medium heat, fry the seasoned kidneys in the hot frying pan for 4–5 minutes, until browned on all sides, then transfer them to the saucepan with the steak.

In the same frying pan, melt half the butter and fry the onion and carrot for 5 minutes, then add them to the saucepan.

Melt the remaining butter in the frying pan and fry the sliced mushrooms for 4 minutes. Add them to the saucepan as well.

Place the large saucepan containing the meat and veg over a medium heat and add the tomato purée and the bay leaf. Stir together, then pour in the hot stock. Bring to the boil, then reduce to a gentle simmer and cook with the lid on for 1–1¼ hours, until the meat is very tender. Check on it every so often, skimming off any scum that rises to the surface. If you think it needs a bit longer cooking, add a splash of water so that the sauce doesn't reduce too much. When it's ready, it should be the consistency of thick gravy.

Remove from the heat, season, to taste, with salt and pepper and add the Worcestershire sauce. Leave to cool to room temperature, then spoon into a 1.2-litre pie dish.

Preheat the oven to 200°C. Roll out the puff pastry to a thickness of about 5mm (it should be large enough to fit over the top of your pie dish with some excess).

Brush beaten egg around the top of the pie dish, then lay the rolled-out pastry over the top, leaving some hanging over the edge. Press the pastry down to seal the pie, and then trim off the excess. Use a fork or the flat side of a knife to crimp all the way round the pastry edge so you have a neat finish. Brush the top of the pie liberally with the rest of the beaten egg. Cook in the oven for 30–40 minutes until the pastry is golden brown. Serve with peas or the red cabbage on page 191.

FILLET OF BEEF 'WELLY'

SERVES 4   PREPARATION TIME: 30 MINUTES   COOKING TIME: 1¼ HOURS

If you want to show off, make a beef Wellington. Hidden underneath the pastry of this version is a secret layer of mushrooms and shallots. Not only will this add extra deliciousness, it will also help stop your meat drying out in the oven.

1 tablespoon vegetable oil
700g beef fillet, trimmed of fat and sinew
butter, for greasing
a little flour, to dust
500g puff pastry
1 egg, beaten
sea salt and pepper

for the mushroom and shallot filling
50g butter
150g shallots, peeled and diced
250g flat mushrooms, roughly chopped
1 teaspoon fresh thyme leaves
150ml dry white wine
1 tablespoon chopped fresh parsley
salt and pepper

First, make the mushroom and shallot filling. Melt the butter in a pan over a medium heat and when it starts to foam, cook the shallots for about 5 minutes, until softened but not coloured. Throw in the chopped mushrooms, thyme leaves and wine and season with salt and pepper. Cook for 8–10 minutes until you are left with a dry mixture. Tip into a food processor and blitz with the parsley. Set aside and leave to cool

Heat the oil in a frying pan. Season the beef all over with lots of salt and pepper. When the oil is very hot, carefully add the beef, searing well all over for 4–5 minutes. Keep turning so it cooks evenly. Remove from the heat.

Preheat the oven to 180°C. Grease a baking tray with butter. Roll out the puff pastry on to a lightly floured work surface until it is about 5mm thick and large enough to wrap around the beef. Brush it all over with the beaten egg, then gently spread the mushroom and shallot mixture all over the pastry, leaving a 3cm border.

Place the seared beef at one of the short ends and carefully roll it over so it's covered in the pastry, with the joins underneath. Trim off any extra pastry – you don't want it doubled over very far if you can avoid it. Use any extra pastry to decorate the top, or you can just make a criss-cross pattern with a sharp knife.

Brush the top with more beaten egg and sprinkle with sea salt. Carefully place the Wellington on the greased baking tray and cook in the oven for 40–45 minutes, until the pastry is golden. Remove from the oven and allow to rest for 5 minutes before carving.

SPICED ROAST LEG OF LAMB
with tzatziki

SERVES 6   PREPARATION TIME: 10 MINUTES   CHILLING TIME: OVERNIGHT
COOKING TIME: 1 HOUR PLUS 15 MINUTES RESTING TIME

This is a brilliant way to get loads of flavour into your lamb. You need to start this recipe the day before so it can marinate overnight. Ask your butcher to prepare the lamb for you so you don't have to bother with it yourself. Serve with salad or couscous.

800g–1kg leg of lamb, boned, rolled and tied
1 lemon halved
1 head of garlic, split in half

for the marinade
2 onions, peeled and roughly chopped
3 garlic cloves, peeled and roughly chopped
1 small bunch of fresh flat-leaf
  parsley leaves
1 bunch of fresh coriander leaves
1 tablespoon chilli powder
2 tablespoons ground cumin
2 tablespoons ground turmeric
2 tablespoons sweet paprika

30g sea salt
100ml olive oil
juice and zest of 1 lemon
1 lemon halved
1 head of garlic, split in half
salt and pepper

for the tzatziki
1 cucumber, peeled, halved lengthways,
  deseeded and diced
2 garlic cloves, peeled and crushed
200g thick Greek yoghurt
75ml extra virgin olive oil
20 fresh mint leaves, roughly chopped
sea salt

Blitz all the marinade ingredients in a food processor until you achieve a fine paste. Season with salt and pepper. Rub the paste all over the lamb, making sure to really work it into the flesh, then place the lamb in a roasting tin and leave to marinate in the fridge overnight.

When you're ready to cook the lamb, preheat the oven to 200°C. Season the lamb with a little more salt and pepper, then roast in the oven for 1 hour, until golden brown all over (this will result in lamb that is a little pink in the middle; if you like it more well done, cook for a further 30 minutes). Place the lemon halves and the split head of garlic in the roasting tray with the lamb, for additional flavour.

For the tzatziki, mix together all the ingredients in a bowl and refrigerate until needed.

When the lamb is cooked, remove it from the oven and leave it to rest, covered in foil, for 15 minutes before carving, and squeeze over the roasted lemon juices. Serve with a generous dollop of tzatziki.

LAMB HOTPOT

SERVES 4   PREPARATION TIME: 30 MINUTES   COOKING TIME: 3–4 HOURS

Cheaper cuts of meat are packed with flavour, all you need is to be patient and inject some love into it. Once you've got it all on the hob, you can just leave it bubbling away while you get on with your life. The extra layer of onions underneath the potatoes gives it a really sweet taste.

750g lamb neck, cut into 2.5cm pieces

plain flour, seasoned with salt and pepper, for dusting

4 tablespoons vegetable oil

20 button onions or shallots, peeled

a few sprigs of fresh thyme

5 medium carrots, peeled and cut into 2.5cm pieces

175ml white wine

1 litre hot chicken or lamb stock

2 white onions, halved and finely sliced

500g Desiree or Maris Piper potatoes, peeled and thinly sliced

1 tablespoon olive oil

salt and pepper

On a large plate, dust the lamb pieces generously with the seasoned flour. Heat 2 tablespoons of the vegetable oil in a large ovenproof saucepan or casserole over a medium to high heat and cook the lamb in two batches, adding another tablespoon of oil if necessary, for 5–10 minutes, until browned on all sides. Transfer to a bowl.

Add the onions and thyme to the hot pan and cook for 4–5 minutes, until lightly coloured. Add the carrot and cook for a further 4 minutes, then add the wine, bring to a simmer and cook for 5 minutes.

Return the lamb to the pan and mix to combine the meat and veg. Pour in the hot stock, making sure it covers everything. Bring to the boil, reduce the heat and simmer for 1½–2 hours, checking on it every half an hour or so and giving it a stir. Keep adding water so that it stays covered. When it is cooked, the meat should be very tender and fall apart when you poke it with a fork, the liquid should have thickened slightly, but still cover everything, and the veg should have started to break down. If it's still quite liquidy, increase the heat and allow to reduce down to a thick gravy.

Meanwhile, heat the remaining tablespoon of vegetable oil in a frying pan over a low to medium heat. Add the onion, season, and cook very gently for 20 minutes, until the slices are sticky and soft. Preheat your oven to 180°C.

When the meat is ready, make a layer of potato slices on top of the stew. Top with a layer of onions, then repeat the layers, finishing with potatoes. Drizzle with olive oil and season. Cover with a tight-fitting lid and cook in the oven for 45 minutes–1 hour, until the potatoes are soft in the middle and the hotpot is crispy and golden on top.

SWEET-AND-SOUR PORK BROTH

with pineapple and bok choy

SERVES 4   PREPARATION TIME: 20 MINUTES   COOKING TIME: 3½ HOURS

If you think of sweet-and-sour, I bet it's that thick gloopy orange sauce that comes from the Chinese! I've taken the flavours that we love from our takeaway favourite, but given them a fresh update in this light and healthy broth.

80g fresh root ginger, sliced and smashed

8 spring onions, cut into 2.5cm lengths (use the white and green parts)

70g palm sugar, chopped, or soft brown sugar

2 star anise

1 cinnamon stick

60ml dry sherry

120ml soy sauce

1.5 litres chicken stock

2.2kg pork shoulder, cut into 2cm dice

300g fresh pineapple, diced

4 small heads of bok choy

2 tablespoons chopped fresh coriander leaves

Put the ginger, half the spring onions, the sugar, star anise, cinnamon stick, sherry, soy sauce and chicken stock into a deep wok. Bring to the boil and simmer for 5–10 minutes so that the sugar dissolves and the flavours infuse.

Add the pork pieces and leave to simmer gently for about 3 hours. The pork should be lovely and tender.

When it is cooked, strain the tasty broth through a sieve into a clean saucepan set over a medium heat. Skim off any fat from the surface. Transfer the cooked pork to a bowl and cover loosely with foil to keep warm. Add the pineapple chunks and the remaining pieces of spring onion to the broth and simmer for 10 minutes. The broth will reduce and have an even more intense flavour.

While the broth is reducing, bring a saucepan of water to the boil and cook the bok choy for about 5 minutes. It should be tender, but still with a bit of bite.

Place some warm bok choy in each serving bowl and top with some of the pork. Spoon over the hot broth and finish with a sprinkle of chopped coriander leaves.

SAUSAGE STEW

SERVES 6   PREPARATION TIME: 10 MINUTES   COOKING TIME: 45–55 MINUTES

Use whatever sausages you like in this hearty stew. If you feel like pork and leek or beef and chilli, then crack on! The bread stirred through at the end soaks up all the lovely rich juices. Just spoon it into bowls and dig in.

6 Cumberland sausages
6 of your favourite sausages
1 tablespoon vegetable oil
150g bacon pieces
1 white onion, peeled and chopped
2 sticks of celery, roughly chopped
2 garlic cloves, peeled and chopped
400g tin of cannellini beans, drained

400g tin of butter beans, drained
400g tin of chopped tomatoes
250ml hot chicken stock
150g day-old loaf (French stick, bloomer or sourdough), torn into rough pieces
2 tablespoons chopped fresh basil
1 tablespoon chopped fresh chives
salt and pepper

Slice all the sausages in half to make 24 short sausages. Heat the oil in a large saucepan over a medium to high heat and, when hot, fry the bacon for a couple of minutes until just starting to colour.

Stir in the onion, celery and garlic and season with a little salt and lots of pepper. Cook for 1 minute, and then add the sausages. Mix everything together and cook for 5 minutes, until the sausages are starting to brown nicely.

Stir in the beans and tomatoes and pour in the hot stock. Stir to combine, then reduce the heat to medium to low and simmer for 35–45 minutes, until the stew is lovely and thick. Just before serving, stir through the bread and fresh herbs.

═ PIG IN A BUN ═

MAKES ENOUGH TO FILL 10 BUNS   PREPARATION TIME: 20 MINUTES   COOKING TIME: 5½–6 HOURS

This is perfect pulled pork without the industrial smokery or hours stoking a barbecue. The pork does take a long time in the oven, but it's important the meat is cooked very slowly so that it's tender and sweet and unbelievably delicious. Pack into buns with plenty of slaw.

4–5kg pork shoulder, neck end
10 buns
1 x quantity of cabbage and apple slaw
  (see page 75)

for the sauce
80g butter
6 tablespoons olive oil
2 shallots, peeled and finely diced
200ml tomato ketchup
80ml French's mustard

100ml apple juice
50ml clear honey
40ml Worcestershire sauce
2 teaspoons Tabasco sauce
2 tablespoons cider vinegar
40g fine salt
100g soft brown sugar
20g smoked paprika
1 teaspoon cayenne pepper

Preheat the oven to 160°C. Melt the butter in a saucepan over a low heat. Add the rest of the sauce ingredients, mixing thoroughly to combine.

Score the pork skin all over with a sharp knife, then place the pork in the middle of a roasting tin. Pour over the sauce and massage it into the pork, really working it into the meat.

Cook in the preheated oven for 5½ to 6 hours, occasionally basting the sauce and juices over the pork whilst it's roasting. When the pork is cooked, it should pull apart easily.

When you're ready to serve, remove any crispy crackling, break it up and set aside as an added extra garnish. Now pull apart the pork, discarding any pieces of bone and fat. Using two forks, shred the pork into strands and place back in the roasting tin. Cover with foil to keep warm. Serve the juicy pork in the buns with plenty of slaw.

FISH PIE

SERVES 4–6   PREPARATION TIME: 15 MINUTES   COOKING TIME: 1¼ HOURS

A great dish to make for a dinner party – just whack it on the table with a load of peas and a big bowl of tartare sauce (see page 118). The sweet potato mash brings a really lovely sweetness and the herby sauce is a great twist on the standard version. I like to chop up the eggs for an extra creamy layer, rather than leaving them whole or cutting them in half. The scallops make it into something special, but you can leave them out if you prefer.

250g Maris Piper potatoes, peeled and halved
250g sweet potatoes, peeled and halved
150ml milk
50g butter
100g Parmesan cheese, grated
320g fish pie mix (haddock, cod, salmon)
150g scallops
150g raw prawns
4 hard-boiled eggs, peeled and roughly chopped

200g peas
salt and pepper

for the herb sauce
1 tablespoon butter
1 shallot, peeled and finely chopped
150ml white wine
500ml single cream
1 tablespoon chopped fresh soft herbs (e.g. chives, parsley and tarragon)
juice of ½ lemon

First make the mash. Bring a large pan of salted water to the boil and cook the potatoes and sweet potatoes for 15–20 minutes, until tender. Place the milk and butter in a small pan and heat over a medium heat until the butter has completely melted. Drain the cooked potatoes, return to the hot pan and mash with the milk and butter until very smooth. (If you have a ricer, now's the time to use it.) Stir through the Parmesan cheese and set aside.

To make the herb sauce, melt the butter in a saucepan over a medium heat until it starts to foam. Add the shallot and cook for 3–4 minutes, until it is just starting to soften. Pour in the wine and let it bubble away until it has reduced by half. Stir through the cream, herbs and lemon juice, then bring to the boil and simmer for 5 minutes.

Preheat the oven to 180°C. Arrange the fish and seafood in an ovenproof dish and scatter over the eggs and peas. Try to spread it all out evenly so everyone gets a bit of everything. Top with the herb sauce, season with salt and pepper and mix gently to coat. Cover with a layer of cheesy mash and cook in the oven for 40–45 minutes, until the potato is nicely glazed and the filling is bubbling up around the edges. Serve with plenty of tartare sauce (see page 118).

≡ SURF AND TURF ≡
grilled veal chops, tuna and caper sauce

SERVES 4   PREPARATION TIME: 15 MINUTES   COOKING TIME: 15 MINUTES

This dish is inspired by the classic Italian dish vitello tonnato – sliced veal with a creamy tuna sauce. It sounds like a bit of a mad combination, but it's really tasty! My version is lighter, using fresh tuna rather than tinned – make sure it's as fresh as you can get it, as it's eaten almost raw.

4 x 340g rose veal chops
   (about 3–4cm thick)
1 tablespoon olive oil
lemon wedges, to serve
salt and pepper

for the sauce
125g salted butter
3 garlic cloves, peeled and sliced into slivers
2 banana shallots, peeled and finely diced
3 tablespoons small capers
1 tablespoon roughly chopped fresh
   flat-leaf parsley
juice and zest of 1 lemon
250g fresh tuna (centre cut), diced into
   5mm pieces

To make the sauce, melt the butter in a saucepan over a low heat and add the garlic slivers and diced shallots. Leave to cook gently for 5 minutes so that the flavours can infuse – be careful not to burn the garlic. Preheat the oven to 160°C.

Season the veal chops all over with salt and pepper. Heat the oil in a frying pan over a medium to high heat and cook the chops for 2–3 minutes on each side, until they have taken on some good colour. Transfer them to a baking tray and finish cooking in the oven for about 5 minutes.

To finish the sauce, stir the capers, chopped parsley, lemon zest and juice into the shallots. Add the diced tuna and mix well so that the hot buttery ingredients coat the fish. Remove from the heat.

Serve the cooked veal chops on warm plates and spoon over the tuna and caper sauce. Garnish with lemon wedges.

GRILLED SALMON
with lettuce, cucumber and tomato

SERVES 4   PREPARATION TIME: 10 MINUTES   COOKING TIME: 10 MINUTES

I've brought the most classically British combination of ingredients – lettuce, cucumber and tomato – bang up to date. The tomato pesto cuts through the richness of the lettuce once it's cooked and the cucumber relish adds a lovely sharp flavour.

2 tablespoons vegetable oil
4 x 150g salmon fillets (skin on)
sea salt

for the sautéed lettuce and tomato
2 Little Gem lettuces
1 tablespoon vegetable oil
2 tablespoons tomato pesto
salt and pepper

for the cucumber relish
½ cucumber, halved lengthways, deseeded and very thinly sliced
1 tablespoon olive oil
1 tablespoon fresh dill
salt

In a small bowl, mix together the ingredients for the cucumber relish and chill in the fridge while you cook the salmon.

Preheat the grill to high. Place a rack in the bottom of a baking tray. Oil the salmon fillets and place them skin side down in the tray, drizzle over the rest of the oil and scatter over some salt. Grill for 8–10 minutes, depending on the thickness, until crispy on top and a little pink in the middle. Eating salmon a little pink is perfectly acceptable and will add delicious texture to the dish.

While the salmon is cooking, chop off the base from each lettuce and pull apart the leaves. Heat the oil in a pan over a medium heat and when it is hot, add the leaves. Season with salt and pepper. Cook them for 2–3 minutes, until they have just wilted. Keep a careful eye on them because you don't want them to burn. They will cook quickly – like spinach. When they have wilted, stir through the tomato pesto.

Serve the lettuce with the salmon and finish with the cucumber relish.

GNOCCHI
with wild mushroom ragù

SERVES 4   PREPARATION TIME: 25 MINUTES   COOKING TIME: 1¼ HOURS

This dish is on the menu at all my restaurants because it's just so popular. It has a perfect balance of flavours, and the truffle oil gives it a touch of luxury. You can speed it up by microwaving the potatoes or buying some ready-made gnocchi.

Mushroom ragù
2 tablespoons vegetable oil
200g wild mushrooms, sliced
16 sundried tomatoes in oil, drained
250ml double cream
50ml Madeira
3 tablespoons sundried tomato pesto
1 tablespoon truffle oil
30g Parmesan cheese, grated

a large handful of fresh spinach leaves
salt and pepper

for the gnocchi
500g Desiree potatoes, unpeeled
300g Tipo 00 pasta flour
200g Parmesan cheese, grated
3 egg yolks
2 garlic cloves, peeled and crushed
plain flour, for dusting

Preheat the oven to 180°C. Bake the potatoes for 45–55 minutes, until they are very soft. Cut them in half and carefully scoop the flesh into a bowl. They will be hot, so use some tea towels to help you hold them. Add the flour, Parmesan, egg yolks and garlic and mix together until completely combined and you have a stiff dough.

Divide the dough into quarters. Using your hands, roll each piece of dough on a lightly floured surface into a sausage shape about 2cm thick. Then cut these into 2.5cm pieces. Place them on a tray (not touching) and chill in the freezer while you make the sauce.

Heat half the oil in a saucepan over a medium heat and fry the mushrooms for 4–5 minutes, until lightly browned. Add the sundried tomatoes next, increase the heat a little and fry for a minute or so, then stir in the cream. Cook for about 30 seconds, then add the Madeira, pesto and truffle oil. Give it a good stir and let it bubble for a couple of minutes to reduce. Season with salt and pepper. Stir in the Parmesan and spinach and set aside while you cook the gnocchi.

Heat the rest of the oil in a clean frying pan over a medium heat and, when hot, fry the gnocchi for 3–4 minutes, until golden brown. Keep turning them so they cook evenly. Transfer the gnocchi to some kitchen roll to drain off any excess oil.

Place the mushroom ragù back over a medium heat and mix through the cooked gnocchi. Heat for a few minutes, then serve.

THREE CHEESE VEGETABLE LASAGNE

SERVES 6   PREPARATION TIME: 30 MINUTES   COOKING TIME: 50 MINUTES–1 HOUR

This rich and creamy lasagne will please even the most meat-loving of meat lovers out there! The three cheeses make it extra luxurious while the roasted veg keep it light. Pre cooking the pasta gives the dish a much smoother texture. Delicious.

1 x quantity of tomato sauce (see page 151)
20 fresh or dried pasta sheets
oil, for the pasta
150g Parmesan cheese, grated
150g goat's cheese
125g buffalo mozzarella, broken into pieces
16 fresh basil leaves

for the béchamel sauce
80g butter
80g plain flour
1.2 litres full-fat milk
150g strong Cheddar cheese, grated

for the roasted vegetables
1 aubergine, cut lengthways into
  1cm-thick slices
100ml olive oil
1 courgette, cut lengthways into
  5mm-thick slices
2 red peppers, halved, deseeded
  and cut into thin strips
2 red onions, peeled and cut into
  2cm-thick wedges
4 sprigs of fresh thyme
2 garlic cloves, peeled and crushed
salt and pepper

Preheat the oven to 200°C. Place the aubergine slices on a baking sheet lined with baking paper. Brush with olive oil. Place the courgette, red pepper and red onion in a separate roasting tin. Drizzle over 2 tablespoons of olive oil and tuck in the thyme and garlic. Season the veg with salt and pepper. Cook in the oven for about 20 minutes until lightly coloured and softened, then set aside to cool.

Meanwhile, make the béchamel. Melt the butter in a small saucepan over a low heat. Sprinkle in the flour and stir together for a couple of minutes until it forms a smooth paste. Increase the heat to medium and gradually pour in the milk, stirring until completely incorporated. Off the heat stir in the Cheddar, then season.

Cook the lasagne sheets in salted boiling water until al dente. Drain pasta, then toss them in oil (to prevent them sticking together) and leave them to cool.

To build the lasagne, spread about a quarter of the béchamel over the base of a 25cm x 32cm baking dish. Follow with a quarter of the roasted vegetables, then a layer of lasagne sheets – the sheets don't need to overlap. Next, spoon over a quarter of the tomato sauce and scatter over some of the Parmesan, goat's and mozzarella cheeses. Dot with a few basil leaves. Repeat three times, finishing with béchamel and topping with the remaining cheeses. Bake for about 30–40 minutes until bubbling and golden.

FOR THE Table

It doesn't have to be complicated, but I do think you need to give a bit of thought to what you serve alongside the main event. This chapter includes a selection of sides – and a few that work as veggie main dishes as well – so you can mix and match with other recipes in the book.

Who can forget how great potato croquettes are for soaking up the escaped juices from a chicken Kiev! There's also my grandma's recipe for the best ever roasties (thanks, Nan!). And this chapter wouldn't be complete without my ultimate triple-cooked chips – I could almost eat them for dinner on their own . . .

- ★ BUBBLE AND SQUEAK WITH DUCK EGGS ★
- ★ ROASTED VEGETABLES ★
- ★ CABBAGE AND BACON WITH CELERIAC AND CARROT ★
- ★ MIXED VEG CURRY WITH PICKLED CUCUMBER ★
- ★ SUNDAY CARROTS ★
- ★ RED CABBAGE ★
- ★ CAULIFLOWER CHEESE WITH A GOLDEN SULTANA CRUST ★
- ★ BOULANGÈRE POTATO BAKE ★
- ★ GRATED ROOT VEG REMOULADE ★
- ★ NAN'S CRISPY ROAST POTATOES ★
- ★ TRIPLE-COOKED CHIPS ★
- ★ POTATO CROQUETTES ★
- ★ PAN-FRIED JERSEY ROYALS, PEAS, BROAD BEANS AND FRESH MINT ★
- ★ BAKED ONIONS WRAPPED IN BACON WITH ROSEMARY ★

BUBBLE AND SQUEAK
with duck eggs

SERVES 4 AS A MAIN COURSE, 6 AS A SIDE   PREPARATION TIME: 10 MINUTES
COOKING TIME: 30 MINUTES

This is a dish straight from my childhood. I remember my nan cooking this for us when we went round to her house after school on a Monday. This version is a bit fancier than the one my nan gave us, but she wouldn't mind that I've given it a bit of a twist! If you're serving it as a side, you may want to skip the egg.

500g Desiree or Maris Piper potatoes, peeled and chopped into 2.5cm chunks
2 carrots, peeled and chopped
250g spring greens or curly kale
2 tablespoons vegetable oil
optional: 150g bacon pieces

4–6 duck eggs (or hens' eggs)
a big bag of rocket leaves
1 tablespoon olive oil
Parmesan cheese shavings, to serve
salt and pepper

Bring a large pan of salted water to the boil and cook the potato and carrot for 15 minutes. Add the spring greens and cook for a further 5 minutes. All the veg should be very soft at this stage. Drain well and mix together gently.

If you're using bacon, heat 1 tablespoon of the vegetable oil in a frying pan and fry it until it starts to colour. If you're not using bacon, heat 1 tablespoon of vegetable oil anyway. Add the potato, carrot and spring greens and season with salt and pepper. Using a fork, gently crush the ingredients and spread them out to form an even layer in the bottom of the pan. Leave for a couple of minutes, so crispy bits form on the base, then mix through again. Repeat a couple more times until the bubble and squeak is well textured with some crunchy bits throughout.

Meanwhile, fry your eggs in the remaining vegetable oil until cooked to your liking.

Just before serving, mix together the rocket with the olive oil and the Parmesan shavings. Top the bubble and squeak with a fried egg and serve with a salad alongside, if you like.

≡ ROASTED VEGETABLES ≡

SERVES 4 AS A MAIN COURSE, 6 AS A SIDE   PREPARATION TIME: 10 MINUTES
COOKING TIME: 45 MINUTES

A hugely versatile dish that may be served hot or cold and can accompany endless meals. Serve it as a main course with some couscous, rice or crusty bread to soak up the juices or as a side with some grilled lamb or a steak. This is quite a summery version, but you can experiment with whatever veg you have to hand. Just make sure to use some meatier veg and cut them all to roughly the same size so that they cook evenly.

6 asparagus spears, woody ends removed and chopped into thirds

6 baby courgettes, halved lengthways (or use 3 normal ones, halved)

180g jar of artichokes in olive oil

1 bulb of fennel, cut into 8 (reserve the tops)

15 cherry tomatoes

zest and juice of 1 lemon

1 tablespoon capers

cracked black pepper

Preheat the oven to 180°C. Arrange all the vegetables in a single layer in a baking dish (you may need to use two dishes). Toss to coat in the oil from the jar of artichokes. Cook in the oven for 45 minutes, until the vegetables are slightly golden and starting to soften.

Just before serving, sprinkle over the lemon zest and juice and scatter over the capers and fennel tops. Season generously with cracked black pepper.

CABBAGE AND BACON
with celeriac and carrot

SERVES 4 AS A MAIN COURSE, 6 AS A SIDE   PREPARATION TIME: 15 MINUTES
COOKING TIME: 45 MINUTES

This is one of those incredibly simple old-school dishes that never lets you down. I've added celeriac to the traditional cabbage recipe for a bit more substance. Celeriac is an unusual-looking vegetable, but don't be put off by its odd appearance – it has a subtle flavour that works well with almost any other ingredient.

2 tablespoons vegetable oil
200g cubes of pancetta
200g celeriac, peeled and chopped
  into 5mm pieces
1 carrot, peeled and thinly sliced

1 medium Savoy cabbage, outer leaves
  discarded, very finely shredded
300ml hot light chicken or vegetable stock
300ml double cream

Heat the oil in a large saucepan over a medium heat and fry the pancetta for 4–5 minutes, until lightly coloured.

Add the celeriac and carrot pieces and cook for 5 minutes, stirring to coat. Add the cabbage and pour in the hot stock. Bring to the boil, then let it simmer for 5 minutes, so that it reduces slightly.

Turn down the heat to low and stir through the cream. Leave for 20–30 minutes, stirring every so often, until the vegetables are soft when poked with a fork and the sauce has thickened and coats the ingredients.

MIXED VEG CURRY
with pickled cucumber

SERVES 4 AS A SIDE, 2 AS A MAIN COURSE   PREPARATION TIME: 15 MINUTES
COOKING TIME: 30 MINUTES

I often think the vegetable curries in Indian restaurants are the most interesting – there are so many amazing ingredients to try! My version uses some classic English vegetables, like asparagus and courgettes, but with coconut milk from Southeast Asia.

1 tablespoon vegetable oil

1 red onion, peeled and chopped

2 garlic cloves, peeled and chopped

2 tablespoons curry paste (your favourite from a jar, or use the recipe on page 146)

6 baby sweetcorn, halved

6 asparagus spears, woody ends removed and chopped into thirds

4 baby courgettes, halved lengthways

1 red pepper, chopped into 2cm dice

200g tin of chopped tomatoes

200ml coconut milk

50g fresh spinach leaves

juice of ½ lemon

25g toasted flaked almonds

1 tablespoon chopped fresh coriander

2 tablespoons natural yoghurt

salt and pepper

for the pickled cucumber

½ cucumber, peeled, halved lengthways, deseeded and very finely sliced

2 tablespoons caster sugar

4 tablespoons white wine vinegar

3 tablespoons olive oil

1 teaspoon chopped fresh dill

salt and pepper

Mix together all the ingredients for the pickled cucumber in a small bowl and leave to marinate in the fridge while you cook the curry.

Heat the oil in a large saucepan over a medium heat and fry the onion and garlic for a couple of minutes, until starting to soften. Stir in the curry paste and cook for another couple of minutes to release the flavours. Your kitchen should smell amazing!

Add the rest of the veg apart from the spinach and stir in the chopped tomatoes and the coconut milk. Bring to a rapid simmer, then lower the heat and simmer for 15–20 minutes, until all the vegetables are tender and the sauce is lovely and thick.

Season, to taste, with salt and pepper, then stir through the spinach and lemon juice. Cook for just a minute more so that the spinach wilts a little.

Serve scattered with the flaked almonds and chopped coriander and drizzle with natural yoghurt. Place a pot of the pickled cucumber on the side or dollop some on top.

≡ SUNDAY CARROTS ≡

SERVES 4–6   PREPARATION TIME: 5 MINUTES   COOKING TIME: 10 MINUTES

Plain boiled carrots can be revolting: watery, flavourless and soggy. We all remember them being served up like this, but thankfully there is another way to carrot perfection! Here is my recipe for failsafe delicious carrots that we serve up every Sunday. The carrots and your dinner guests will thank you.

6 large carrots, peeled and chopped into rough 2.5cm pieces

150ml orange cordial (e.g. Robinsons squash)

1 teaspoon salt

4 bay leaves

1 teaspoon cumin seeds

optional: 2 cloves

50g butter

2 tablespoons honey

1 tablespoon chopped fresh chives

juice of ½ lemon

salt and pepper

Place the carrots in a saucepan and pour over the cordial and enough water to just cover them. Add the salt, bay leaves, cumin seeds and cloves (if using). Bring to the boil over a medium heat, then lower the heat and simmer the carrots for 5–6 minutes, or until tender. Drain and discard the flavourings.

Melt the butter in a frying pan over a medium heat until it starts to foam. Toss the carrots in the melted butter, then stir through the honey, chives and lemon juice. Season, to taste, with salt and pepper.

RED CABBAGE

SERVES 6   PREPARATION TIME: 10 MINUTES   COOKING TIME: 2–2¼ HOURS

This is a very simple side dish, but you need to make sure all the ingredients play their part. Shred the cabbage as finely as you can – use a mandolin or the shredder on a food processor. If you don't have one just slice very finely.

50g butter
1 red onion, peeled and grated
1 Braeburn apple (unpeeled), grated
a few sprigs of fresh thyme
600g red cabbage, finely shredded
300ml red wine

300ml cider vinegar
300ml fresh orange juice
300ml light chicken stock
a pinch of salt
150g brown sugar
2 tablespoons redcurrant jelly

Melt the butter in a large saucepan over a medium heat. When it starts to foam, add the onion, apple and thyme. Cook gently for 6–8 minutes, to release the juices from the apple and to soften the onion. Don't rush this part; if it takes a few minutes longer, go with it.

Add the cabbage and mix to coat, then pour in the wine, vinegar, orange juice and stock (the cabbage should be completely covered in the liquid). Season with a good pinch of salt, then stir in the sugar. Bring to the boil, then reduce to a simmer and cook for 1½–2 hours, stirring regularly, until the liquid has reduced right down. The cabbage should be completely tender with an almost marmalade consistency. Just before serving, stir through the redcurrant jelly to give it a lovely shine.

CAULIFLOWER CHEESE
with a golden sultana crust

There's something very comforting about cauliflower cheese and this version, with its golden sultana crust, is particularly sweet and moreish. Serve it alongside something simple, like chicken or a steak, for a quick midweek meal.

1 large cauliflower, broken into florets

for the béchamel sauce
50g butter
4 tablespoons plain flour
500ml full-fat milk
100g strong Cheddar cheese, grated
salt and pepper

for the crust
150g fresh breadcrumbs
75g Parmesan cheese, grated
1 teaspoon fresh thyme leaves
3 tablespoons golden sultanas or raisins

Preheat the oven to 180°C. Bring a large pan of salted water to the boil and add the cauliflower florets. Bring back to the boil and cook for 4–5 minutes, until they are soft. Tip them into a colander or sieve to drain and let the steam evaporate.

Meanwhile, make the béchamel. Melt the butter in a small saucepan over a low heat. Sprinkle in the flour and stir together for a couple of minutes until it forms a smooth paste. Increase the heat to medium and pour in the milk a little at a time, stirring between each addition until completely incorporated. Remove from the heat and stir in the Cheddar, then season, to taste, with salt and pepper.

Tip the cauliflower into an ovenproof dish – it should fit snugly in a single layer. Pour over the béchamel and stir to coat.

Mix together the ingredients for the crust and scatter over the top. Bake in the oven for 30–40 minutes until golden brown.

BOULANGÈRE POTATO BAKE

SERVES 4 AS A SIDE   PREPARATION TIME: 20 MINUTES   COOKING TIME: 1½ HOURS

A great all-rounder side dish that goes really well with some simply cooked meat or fish. Try it with breaded lamb cutlets, (page 133) some steamed fish or even a classic roast chicken.

2 tablespoons vegetable oil

3 white onions, peeled and very finely sliced

750g Maris Piper potatoes, peeled

60g butter

1 tablespoon fresh thyme leaves, plus a few to garnish

200ml chicken stock

salt and pepper

Heat the oil in a frying pan over a low heat. Add the onion and season with salt and pepper. Cook very gently for 20–30 minutes – you want the onion to be soft and caramelized, with a sticky consistency almost like onion marmalade.

While the onion is cooking, slice the potatoes *very* thinly. Use a mandolin or the slicing attachment on a food processor if you have one. The potatoes need to be so thin that they're almost transparent. Place them in a bowl.

When the onion is ready and the potatoes are sliced, melt the butter in a small saucepan and add the thyme leaves. Reserving 1 tablespoon, pour the butter over the potatoes and mix gently to coat them.

Preheat the oven to 180°C. Using a pastry brush, grease a square baking dish (25cm x 25cm x 4cm) with half of the reserved melted butter. Line the bottom of the dish with a layer of potato slices, overlapping them slightly. Cover this with a layer of onion. Continue layering in this order, finishing with a layer of potato.

Brush with the remaining butter, then pour in the stock until it starts to appear at the edges of the dish (you may not need it all). Season with salt and pepper and cover with a sheet of greaseproof paper. Place a small dish on top to weigh it down, then cook in the oven for 1 hour, until the top is sticky and a rich golden brown. Finish by garnishing with a few thyme leaves.

GRATED ROOT VEG REMOULADE

You *can* grate the veg by hand, but if you have a shredder or grating attachment on a food processor, I suggest you use it!

2 carrots, peeled and grated
200g celeriac, peeled and grated
100g turnips, peeled and grated

juice of 1 lemon
100g mayonnaise
2 teaspoons wholegrain mustard

Simply combine all the ingredients in a bowl and mix to coat in the dressing.

NAN'S CRISPY ROAST POTATOES

SERVES 4–6   PREPARATION TIME: 10 MINUTES   COOKING TIME: 1 HOUR 10 MINUTES

Everyone loves a good roastie with their Sunday lunch, and this recipe is just like my nan used to make. She usually used beef dripping, but I prefer duck fat. It's up to you, though – vegetable oil will do the job too!

1kg Maris Piper potatoes, peeled and halved

200g duck fat or beef dripping or 200ml vegetable oil

6 garlic cloves, peeled and roughly chopped

zest of 1 lemon

3 sprigs of fresh rosemary, leaves picked

6 anchovies

optional: 1 teaspoon fennel seeds

salt

Place the potatoes in a large saucepan of salted water over a medium heat. Bring to the boil and cook them for 10 minutes, until they are just tender and starting to break up. Drain through a colander and then give them a good shake to fluff the edges. This is what will give you those lovely crispy bits.

Meanwhile, pour the fat into a deep roasting tin and heat in the oven at 200°C.

Using a pestle and mortar (or just chop and mix together on your chopping board), pound the garlic, lemon zest, rosemary, anchovies and fennel seeds (if using) to a paste.

Carefully remove the roasting tin from the oven and add the potatoes. Use a spoon to stir through the paste and coat the potatoes evenly. Cook in the oven for 1 hour, turning every 20 minutes or so.

TRIPLE-COOKED CHIPS

SERVES 4   PREPARATION TIME: 15 MINUTES   CHILLING TIME: 40 MINUTES
COOKING TIME: 30 MINUTES

A good chip is one of life's greatest pleasures. On their own, dipped in sauces, next to a steak, some fish, with a burger – however you like them, you can't go wrong with these extra-crunchy triple-cooked chips.

900g Desiree or Maris Piper potatoes, peeled and cut into thick chips

vegetable oil, for deep-frying
sea salt

Bring a large pan of salted water to the boil and add the chipped potatoes. Return to the boil and simmer for 10 minutes, until they are tender when poked with a fork.

Drain the chips in a colander and let the steam evaporate. Leave them to cool for 10 minutes (the steam evaporating will make them drier and better for frying).

Heat the oil in a deep-fat fryer to 150°C. If you don't have a deep-fat fryer, pour the oil into a deep heavy-based pan and heat over a medium heat until a small cube of bread dropped into the hot oil fizzes and turns golden brown in about 45 seconds.

Carefully lower the chips into the oil and fry for about 5 minutes, until a very light skin is formed. Remove from the oil, drain and leave them to come to room temperature (this will take about 30 minutes).

Bring the oil up to 190°C. This time, a cube of bread dropped into the oil should fizz and turn brown in just 30 seconds. Carefully lower the twice-cooked chips into the hot oil and cook for 3–4 minutes until crispy and golden brown.

Transfer to some kitchen roll to drain off the excess oil and scatter generously with salt.

You will probably need to cook the chips in batches, depending on the size of your fryer or pan. You don't want to overcrowd the pan as this will reduce the temperature of the oil, resulting in soggy, uncooked chips. Keep them warm in a low oven while you cook the rest.

POTATO CROQUETTES

SERVES 4–6 (MAKES 10–12)   PREPARATION TIME: 20 MINUTES
CHILLING TIME: 30 MINUTES OR OVERNIGHT   COOKING TIME: 45 MINUTES

Who remembers having bags of these in the freezer? I certainly do. Make your own and you can add your own flavours (see the black pudding version on page 130). They are perfect for soaking up sauces – or just dipping in ketchup . . .

500g Desiree or Maris Piper potatoes, peeled and cut in half
2 tablespoons butter
½ tablespoon wholegrain mustard
1 tablespoon finely chopped fresh chives
40–50ml double cream

flour, for dusting
1 egg, beaten
50g dry breadcrumbs
3 tablespoons vegetable oil
salt

First make the mash. Bring a large pan of salted water to the boil and cook the potatoes for 15–20 minutes, until tender. Drain, then return the potatoes to the hot pan and mash with some salt until smooth. (If you have a ricer, now's the time to use it.)

Mix through the butter, mustard and chives and enough cream to give an even, smooth consistency, but still hold its shape. It needs to be moulded into croquettes so it can't be at all runny.

Shape into 10 evenly sized balls, then roll each ball into a sausage shape about 7cm long. Place the croquettes on a plate and chill in the fridge for 30 minutes, or overnight.

Preheat the oven to 180°C. Tip the flour into a shallow bowl, the egg into another bowl and the breadcrumbs into a third. Roll the croquettes first in the flour, then the egg and finally the breadcrumbs. Press the crumbs into the croquettes, making sure they are evenly coated.

Heat half the oil in a frying pan over a medium to high heat and cook half the croquettes for 2–3 minutes on each side, turning often, until the crumbs are golden and crispy. Transfer to a baking tray while you fry the remaining croquettes in the rest of the oil. Cook in the oven for 10–15 minutes so they are hot all the way through.

PAN-FRIED JERSEY ROYALS
with peas, broad beans and fresh mint

SERVES 4–6   PREPARATION TIME: 15 MINUTES   COOKING TIME: 30 MINUTES

A bit of a mishmash of veg that makes a great side for some simply cooked chicken or lamb. There's loads going on in here, so you don't need to make a huge effort with the rest of your dinner.

500g Jersey Royal potatoes, scrubbed but not peeled
200g podded broad beans
2 tablespoons olive oil
200g wild mushrooms

200g peas
juice of ½ lemon
10 fresh mint leaves, roughly chopped
salt and pepper

Boil the potatoes in large pan of salted water for 15–20 minutes until tender. Drain well.

Meanwhile, bring a saucepan of salted water to the boil and cook the broad beans for 3 minutes. Drain and cool under cold running water. Slip the beans out of their outer skins, tip into a bowl and set aside.

Heat the oil in a large frying pan over a medium heat. Add the mushrooms and stir-fry for about 3 minutes to colour lightly. Add the cooked potatoes, the peas and beans and toss together. Cook for 5 minutes, stirring regularly. The mushrooms will have released some of their liquids, so you shouldn't need to add any more, but if it's looking a bit dry, splash in a little water.

Just before serving, stir through the lemon juice and mint leaves and season with salt and pepper.

BAKED ONIONS WRAPPED IN BACON
with rosemary

SERVES 4   PREPARATION TIME: 15 MINUTES   COOKING TIME: 1 HOUR

A really old-fashioned dish that I love to eat with fish. The onions will swell up when you cook them, so make sure you fix the bacon on really well. They take a while to cook, but the onions are so sweet and delicious it will be well worth the wait.

4 white onions

30g butter

4–6 sprigs of fresh rosemary
(they need to be quite woody)

8 rashers of thin-cut smoked streaky bacon

2 tablespoons olive oil

salt and pepper

Preheat the oven to 180°C. Keeping the root intact, peel the onions. Cut a cross, 2cm deep, in the top of each onion and squeeze in a knob of butter.

Leaving a few leaves at the end of each sprig of rosemary, pick off and reserve the rest of the leaves.

Wrap two rashers of bacon firmly around each onion. Skewer all the loose ends of bacon to the outer layer of onion, using the rosemary sprigs to hold everything in place (you may need to break off bits of the stem and use them), then arrange in an ovenproof dish.

Drizzle with oil, scatter over the reserved rosemary leaves and season with salt and pepper. Cover the dish tightly with foil and bake in the oven for 1 hour, uncovering for the final 15 minutes, until the onions are soft and tender and a lovely golden colour.

SWEET-
SHOP
Raiders

Ahhhh, jelly, trifle and sticky sponge puddings! This chapter is the ultimate in guilt-free retro comfort food!

In these recipes I've taken the best bits from all our favourite childhood desserts, but I've given them a bit of a grown-up twist – a splash of vodka in a watermelon sorbet or some home-made jam in your roly-poly pudding. This is old-school eating at its best.

There are also some classic recipes for ice cream and custard that you can make to serve alongside your favourite puds.

★ NAN'S TOO-BOOZY TRIFLE ★

★ REAL STRAWBERRY JELLY AND PROPER VANILLA ICE CREAM ★

★ INDIVIDUAL BAKED ALASKAS ★

★ WATERMELON VODKA SORBET ★

★ LAZY CHOCOLATE-CHERRY LAYERED MOUSSE ★

★ PEACH MELBA SUNDAES ★

★ TOFFEE PECAN NUT APPLES ★

★ PLUM AND APPLE WITH OATY NUT CRUMBLE ★

★ BANANA AND WALNUT STICKY SPONGE PUDDING ★

★ RHUBARB AND CUSTARD DOUGHNUTS ★

★ DOUBLE CHOCOLATE SOUFFLÉS WITH ORANGE AND GINGER CONFIT ★

★ RICE PUDDING WITH FRUIT RIPPLES ★

★ SARA LEE INSPIRED MANDARIN CHEESECAKE ★

★ JAM ROLY-POLY ★

★ WELSH CAKES WITH ORANGE AND BASIL MASCARPONE ★

NAN'S TOO-BOOZY TRIFLE

This needs to be started at least a day ahead, but the flavour gets better and better, so if you can get yourself organized, try to start it a couple of days before you need it and it will be perfect. My nan used to make this for me because I didn't like Christmas pudding. She'd make it with Swiss roll in the bottom and she'd always over-whip the cream, so I'd eat it with custard instead!

4 tablespoons raspberry jam

150g amaretti biscuits or sponge fingers

6 tablespoons sweet sherry

200g fruit of your choice – blueberries, strawberries, and raspberries work well

275ml double cream

1½ tablespoons icing sugar

2 tablespoons hundreds-and-thousands

for the custard

150ml whipping cream

150ml milk

½ vanilla pod, sliced lengthways

4 egg yolks

2 tablespoons caster sugar

fresh mint leaves, to garnish

Make the custard by boiling the whipping cream with the milk and vanilla pod in a small saucepan. Leave to cool to room temperature.

Whisk the egg yolks and caster sugar until pale. Pour the cream on to the whisked egg yolks, whisk to combine, then pour back into the same saucepan and cook on a low heat, stirring gently, until it thickens and coats the back of a spoon.

Heat the jam for 2 minutes in a small saucepan over a low heat.

Meanwhile, break the biscuits into the bottom of a glass serving bowl (one of those fancy cut-glass ones would be ideal!). Pour over the sherry and let it soak into the biscuits. Next, pile in the fresh fruit and pour the warmed jam over the top.

When the custard is ready, cover the soaked biscuits and fruit in it and leave the trifle in the fridge overnight to set.

The next day, whip the double cream with the icing sugar until it forms soft peaks. Spoon it into a piping bag and pipe whipped-cream rosettes all over the surface of the custard. Sprinkle with hundreds-and-thousands and chill for at least 1 hour before serving.

REAL STRAWBERRY JELLY
and proper vanilla ice cream

SERVES 6   PREPARATION TIME: 30 MINUTES (PLUS TIME TO MAKE THE ICE CREAM)
CHILLING TIME: 4 HOURS OR OVERNIGHT   COOKING TIME: 10 MINUTES

Jelly and ice cream always puts a smile on everyone's face! And what is a more classic combination than strawberry and vanilla? Here, the jelly is made from real strawberry juice and the vanilla ice cream is rich and luxurious. None of those sickly sweet sticky jelly cubes or that watery ice cream here.

for the jelly
500g strawberries
150g caster sugar
5 leaves of gelatine

for the ice cream
300ml milk

300ml double cream
1 vanilla pod, sliced lengthways and seeds scraped
3 egg yolks
100g sugar

small jelly moulds, ice-cream maker

First, make the jelly. Slice the strawberries in half (reserving a few for a garnish) and tip them into a saucepan. Scatter over the sugar and add 250ml water. Heat over a medium heat and allow to gently boil for 4–5 minutes, so the fruit starts to break down and release all its lovely flavour.

Pass the soft fruit through a fine sieve into a jug, pushing the strawberries through with the back of a spoon or a ladle. Discard the seeds and pulp in the sieve.

Soak the gelatine leaves in a small bowl of cold water for 5 minutes. Remove the leaves and squeeze out the water. Whisk the gelatine through the strawberry juice and pour into your jelly moulds. Dice the reserved strawberries and drop them into the moulds. Chill in the fridge and allow to set fully (this will take at least 4 hours, but ideally leave them overnight).

To make the ice cream, bring the milk and cream with the vanilla pod (seeds and pod as well) to the boil over a medium heat. Meanwhile, whisk together the egg yolks and sugar. Remove the vanilla pod from the pan and pour the hot milk and cream straight on to the eggs, whisking all the time to combine. Chill the mixture in the fridge until it is cold, then transfer to your ice-cream maker and churn until it is nice and soft (ice-cream makers will have different timings, so check yours for instructions).

Turn out the jellies from their moulds and serve with a scoop of ice cream. I find ice cream will never sit on a plate, so if you're trying to impress, a good trick is to crumble a bit of digestive biscuit and sit the ice cream on top.

INDIVIDUAL BAKED ALASKAS

SERVES 6   PREPARATION TIME: 30 MINUTES   CHILLING TIME: 1 HOUR   COOKING TIME: 35 MINUTES

These are always such a spectacle when you serve them up, but they're actually pretty simple to make. It's easier if you have a kitchen blowtorch so you can 'bake' them evenly all over, but it's not too tricky to do under the grill – just keep an eye on them.

150g fresh raspberries
20g icing sugar
6 scoops of vanilla ice cream
  (see page 213)

for the sponge
40g butter
3 eggs
100g caster sugar
100g plain flour, sifted

for the meringue
180g caster sugar
1½ teaspoons liquid glucose
3 egg whites
a squeeze of lemon

stainless steel bowl, sugar thermometer, 6cm-round cutter, kitchen blowtorch

First, make the sponge base by melting the butter in a small saucepan over a low heat. Set aside to cool a little. Line a baking tray with parchment paper. Preheat the oven to 200°C.

Bring a saucepan of water to the boil. Put the eggs and sugar in a stainless steel bowl and set it over the pan of simmering water – make sure the bottom of the bowl doesn't actually touch the water. Whisk hard until the mixture turns pale, creamy and thick.

Remove from the heat and gently fold in the sifted flour. Drizzle in the cooled melted butter and fold into the mixture. Carefully pour on to the lined tray, spreading gently with a palette knife until smooth – it should be about 1cm thick.

Bake in the preheated oven for about 10 minutes, until golden on top and firm to the touch. Leave to cool for 5 minutes, then tip onto a wire rack, peeling off the baking parchment.

While the sponge cools, make the meringue. Place the sugar, liquid glucose and 3 tablespoons of water in a small saucepan and dissolve over a low heat. When the mixture is clear, increase the heat and boil until the syrup reaches 120°C (use a sugar thermometer to test).

While the sugar syrup is heating, whisk the egg whites with a squeeze of lemon juice until they form just-firm peaks. Gently and carefully pour in the hot sugar syrup and continue whisking hard for at least 10 minutes, until the egg whites have become firm and glossy (use an electric whisk to save your energy!). Set aside.

Place the raspberries in a bowl and sift over the icing sugar. Crush the fruit lightly with a fork, then set aside.

Using a 6cm-round cutter, cut out 12 discs from the cooled sponge. Place half the discs on a baking tray and spread with the crushed raspberries. Scoop ice cream on top, then finish each one with another sponge disc.

Quickly cover the whole surface of the ice cream sponges with the meringue, swirling it with a palette knife for decoration.

Chill in the freezer for 1 hour, until ready to serve. Remove from the freezer and place the Alaskas on serving plates, glazing slightly with a blowtorch just before serving (or put under a hot grill for 2–3 minutes until lightly glazed).

WATERMELON VODKA SORBET

A grown-up twist on a summer treat. You can make this in any quantities, but you just need to be careful not to add too much vodka as it won't freeze properly. The rule is one part vodka to eight parts watermelon – top up with a bit of water if you need to.

1.4kg watermelon
sugar syrup (see page 38)
zest and juice of 1 lime

75ml vodka
salt

Cut the watermelon into smallish pieces and slice off the skin. Blitz the flesh in a food processor until completely liquid. Pass the watermelon juice through a fine sieve into a jug to remove any bits. You should end up with 500ml juice. If it's a bit under, top it up with a splash of water.

Stir in the sugar syrup, to taste, lime juice and zest, vodka and a pinch of salt.

Place the mixture in a freezer-proof container with a lid and chill in the freezer for 45 minutes. Take it out of the freezer and give it a good stir to break it all up – scrape around the edges too. Put the lid back on and freeze for another couple of hours, when your sorbet will be ready and delicious.

LAZY CHOCOLATE-CHERRY LAYERED MOUSSE

SERVES 6   PREPARATION TIME: 20 MINUTES   CHILLING TIME: 15 MINUTES
COOKING TIME: 5 MINUTE

This is the laziest pudding going, but sometimes you just want something sweet and chocolatey to round off a meal and this presses all the buttons. In essence, these are the typical blackforest gâteau flavours that we all love. Who remembers how great it was eating cherry pie filling straight from the tin? Go on, you know you do . . .

6 tablespoons tinned cherry pie filling
200g good-quality chocolate brownie
dark chocolate shavings, to garnish
6 fresh cherries, to garnish

for the chocolate mousse
130g dark chocolate, broken into pieces
4 eggs, separated
4 tablespoons sugar syrup (see page 38)

for the cream topping
250ml double cream
2 tablespoons icing sugar
½ teaspoon vanilla extract
1 tablespoon sweet sherry (or Kirsch)

To make the mousse, first melt the chocolate in a heatproof bowl set over a pan of simmering water. Make sure the bottom of the bowl doesn't touch the hot water. Stir gently until completely melted – it should take about 5 minutes. Remove from the heat and leave to cool a little. Stir in the egg yolks and give it all a good mix.

In a clean bowl, whisk the egg whites until they form soft peaks. Then whisk in the sugar syrup. Using a metal spoon, fold the egg white mixture into the chocolate mixture, making sure you get lots of air into it.

Now make the cream topping by whipping the cream with the icing sugar, vanilla and sherry. It should be lovely and light.

To assemble, spoon the cherry pie filling into serving dishes. Top with a layer of chocolate mousse, then some of the whipped cream. Finish by crumbling over some brownie, sprinkling with shaved chocolate and topping with a fresh cherry!

PEACH MELBA SUNDAES

**SERVES 4   PREPARATION TIME: 30 MINUTES (PLUS TIME TO MAKE THE ICE CREAM)
COOLING TIME: 1 HOUR   COOKING TIME: 20 MINUTES**

Pile them high in knickerbocker glory glasses and stick a chocolate straw in the top! These are for birthdays, holidays or whenever you fancy something sweet.

2 fresh ripe peaches (preferably white)
175g caster sugar
275ml white wine
½ vanilla pod, sliced lengthways
450g fresh raspberries

8 small scoops of vanilla ice cream
 (see page 213)
4 tuile biscuits
4 fresh mint sprigs

Bring a saucepan of water to the boil over a medium heat. Drop in the peaches and leave for exactly 10 seconds. Carefully lift them out, allow them to cool until you can handle them, then peel off their skins. Cut them in half and remove and discard the stones.

Place the sugar, wine and vanilla pod in another small saucepan. Bring to the boil over a medium heat, then reduce the heat and simmer for 5 minutes. Add the peach halves and cook gently for 10 minutes. Remove from the heat and leave them to cool in the syrup.

When the peaches are cool, remove them from the syrup and set aside. Place the pan with the syrup over a medium heat and cook until it has reduced by half. Remove from the heat and stir in 150g of the raspberries until they are coated in the syrup. Tip into a food processor or blender and blitz to a smooth sauce. Pass through a sieve to remove the seeds, then leave to cool completely in the fridge.

Chill four sundae glasses in the freezer for 30 minutes while you make the ice cream. If you made the ice cream earlier, remove it from the freezer so it softens slightly. Beat through 150g of raspberries using a wooden spoon or a spatula. Some will break up, others will completely purée and some will escape and stay whole.

To serve, cut each peach half into three pieces. Place a scoop of raspberry ripple ice cream in the bottom of each glass and scatter over three of the peach pieces and a few of the remaining whole raspberries. Spoon over some of the raspberry syrup. Top with another scoop of ice cream, a few more raspberries, a little more syrup and finish with a tuile biscuit and a sprig of fresh mint. A beautiful retro dessert!

TOFFEE PECAN NUT APPLES

MAKES 4   PREPARATION TIME: 10 MINUTES   COOLING TIME: 1 HOUR   COOKING TIME: 10 MINUTES

A slightly more grown-up version of that brilliant fairground treat. But only slightly... Make sure you chop the nuts nice and finely.

4 eating apples (e.g. Braeburn), washed and patted dry
200g soft brown sugar
2 tablespoons golden syrup

25g butter
4 tablespoons pecan nuts, finely chopped
4 wooden lollipop sticks

Remove the stalks from the apples and insert a wooden lollipop stick halfway into each one.

Place the sugar and 50ml water in a saucepan and heat gently over a low heat until the sugar has completely dissolved. Add the golden syrup and the butter, increase the heat to medium, stir gently and bring to the boil. Allow to boil for 4–5 minutes, until it is a dark rich caramel, then remove from the heat.

Spread the nuts over a sheet of greaseproof paper. Dip each apple into the toffee, then roll in the nuts, making sure they are well coated all over. Set aside to cool and let the toffee harden. I find the best way is to stand them upside-down on a sheet of greaseproof paper.

PLUM AND APPLE
with oaty nut crumble

SERVES 6   PREPARATION TIME: 25 MINUTES   COOKING TIME: 50 MINUTES

Apple crumble is such a classic pud, but I've added some plums into the mix here to give it an extra sweetness. The crumble itself is made from nuts and oats so it has a great crunch.

400g Bramley apples
500g plums, halved and de-stoned
40g butter
50g caster sugar
zest of 1 lemon
1 x quantity of custard, to serve
  (see page 208)

for the crumble
100g butter
175g plain flour
75g demerara sugar
40g rolled oats
40g nibbed almonds

Preheat the oven to 180°C. First make the crumble mixture by rubbing the butter into the flour in a bowl until it has a breadcrumb consistency. Next, add the sugar, oats and almonds and mix again until the breadcrumbs become large lumps.

Sprinkle on to a baking sheet, then bake in the preheated oven for about 15 minutes, turning occasionally until crunchy and golden brown.

Meanwhile, peel, quarter and core the apples, then cut each wedge into three pieces. Cut the de-stoned plums into quarters.

Melt the butter in a deep saucepan over a medium heat and when it starts to foam, add the apple, sugar and lemon zest. Cook for about 5 minutes, until the apple begins to soften, then add the plums and cook for a further 10 minutes.

Spoon the cooked fruit into an ovenproof dish and sprinkle the crumble mix over the top. Bake for 15 minutes, then serve with warm custard.

BANANA AND WALNUT STICKY SPONGE PUDDING

SERVES 4   PREPARATION TIME: 30 MINUTES   COOLING TIME: 20 MINUTES   COOKING TIME: 45 MINUTES

Sponge pudding is such a comforting dessert. This recipe includes bananas and walnuts for some added texture. Serve with loads of warm custard.

350g dates, chopped
3 teaspoons bicarbonate of soda
80g caster sugar
80g dark brown sugar
160g demerara sugar
100g butter, plus extra to grease
4 eggs

350g plain flour
60g baking powder
4 bananas, peeled and chopped into small pieces
150g walnuts, chopped roughly
1 x quantity of custard, to serve (see page 208)

Boil the kettle and pour 600ml hot water over the dates in a shallow bowl. Stir in the bicarbonate of soda and cover with clingfilm. Leave to cool completely, then blitz in a food processor to a smooth purée.

Beat together the sugars and the butter until light and fluffy (you can use a food processor if you have one, to make life easier).

Add the eggs and continue to beat until smooth. Fold in the flour and baking powder and beat again until there aren't any lumps.

Stir in the chopped bananas, the walnuts and the cooled date purée mix until evenly combined.

Preheat the oven to 160°C. Grease four ramekins with a little butter and tip the mixture into them. Place in a deep roasting tin and pour hot water to come about halfway up the sides of the ramekins. Cook in the oven for 45 minutes, until the sponge is firm but still a little springy on top. Check they are cooked all the way through by inserting a skewer into the middle; it should come out clean.

Serve with plenty of custard or cream.

RHUBARB AND CUSTARD DOUGHNUTS

MAKES 12 DOUGHNUTS   PREPARATION TIME: 1 HOUR   RESTING TIME: 1¼ HOURS   COOKING TIME: 30 MINUTES

Rhubarb and custard sweets are brilliantly retro – and what a great combination of flavours! Genius. Here, I'll show you how to make an indulgent treat that will remind you of those lovely old-fashioned sweet shops. (I've given you the instructions for making crème pâtissière but, between you and me, there's absolutely nothing wrong with shop-bought custard and, in fact, it sometimes works even better than the home-made stuff!)

225g plain flour, plus extra for dusting
1 tablespoon fast-acting yeast
¼ teaspoon salt
1 tablespoon caster sugar, plus
  extra for dusting
150ml warm milk
30g butter, melted
1 egg yolk, beaten
300ml vegetable oil, for frying

for the rhubarb jam
300g rhubarb, chopped into 5cm lengths
200g sugar
juice of ½ orange

for the custard
4 medium egg yolks
50g caster sugar
20g plain flour
3 level teaspoons cornflour
350ml milk
1 teaspoon vanilla extract

Sift the flour into a large bowl and mix in the yeast, salt and sugar. Make a well in the flour and pour in the warm milk, melted butter and the beaten egg yolk. Using your hands, mix to form a dough, then knead for about 10 minutes, until the dough feels elastic. Cover the bowl with clingfilm and leave to stand for about 45 minutes, until the dough has doubled in size.

Meanwhile, make the rhubarb jam. Place all the ingredients in a saucepan and heat gently over a medium heat for about 20 minutes, until you have a smooth rhubarb purée. Stir frequently and keep an eye on it so that it doesn't catch and burn on the bottom. Use a whisk to help break down the rhubarb. Leave to cool. (If you have any left over, it's great served with ice cream or yoghurt or on top of your muesli.)

Now, make the custard. In a large bowl, whisk together the egg yolks and sugar until light and frothy. Whisk in the flour and cornflour and set aside. Place the milk and vanilla extract in a saucepan and bring to the boil over a low heat. Remove the pan from the heat and leave to cool for a couple of minutes. Pour the hot milk mixture onto the egg mixture, whisking continuously, then return to the pan. Bring the mixture back to the boil and simmer for 2 minutes, whisking all the time, until the custard has thickened. Pour into a bowl and leave to cool while you finish the doughnuts.

On a floured work surface, knead the dough for 5 minutes, then divide into 12 evenly sized pieces. Knead each piece for 2 minutes, then form into balls. Place the dough balls on a tray, with plenty of space around them, cover with clingfilm and leave them to rest in a warm place for 30 minutes, until they have doubled in size.

Heat the oil in a deep-fat fryer to 190°C. (Alternatively, pour the oil into a large, deep pan set over a medium heat. Test the temperature by dropping in a small cube of bread; if it floats and turns golden within about 30 seconds, it is hot enough.) Be very careful, as hot oil can be dangerous. Never leave it unattended.

Gently lower the dough balls into the hot oil in batches of two or three and fry them for 3–5 minutes, until golden brown, then carefully turn them over and fry for a further couple of minutes. Using a slotted spoon, carefully remove the doughnuts from the hot oil and drain on kitchen roll.

Fill a piping bag (or a freezer bag with the corner snipped off) with the rhubarb jam. Cut a small hole in a doughnut with a sharp knife and remove a bit of the inside to make room for the filling. Pipe a small amount into the centre of each doughnut, then repeat with the custard, using another piping bag. Push the bit of dough you cut out back in to seal, then roll the doughnuts in plenty of sugar.

DOUBLE CHOCOLATE SOUFFLÉS
with orange and ginger confit

SERVES 4   PREPARATION TIME: 30 MINUTES   COOKING TIME: 30 MINUTES

This is a special recipe for me because it's what I made when I won a big competition that really kick-started my cooking career. It was the Springboard FutureChef competition when I was 15 and ever since then I've never looked back.

a little butter, for greasing
295g caster sugar
60g dark chocolate, broken into small
   pieces
65g plain flour
60g cocoa powder
3 egg whites

for the orange and ginger confit
3 oranges
150g caster sugar
1 tsp grated fresh root ginger

First, make the fiery orange and ginger confit. Peel and segment the oranges, pouring any juice into a cup. Tip the sugar into a small saucepan and pour over 50ml water. Bring to the boil over a low heat and swirl gently until the sugar has completely dissolved. Add the grated ginger and the orange segments and juice. Cook for 1 minute, stirring gently, then remove from the heat and set aside.

Preheat the oven to 190°C. Grease 4 ramekins with a little butter. Place 250g sugar in a small pan and add 150ml water. Bring to the boil over a medium heat. Once it's boiling, carefully whisk in the chocolate until melted, then set aside.

In a bowl, mix together the flour, cocoa powder and 250ml water. Now add this to the pan of water, sugar and chocolate and using a spatula stir constantly over a medium heat until really thick, it should take 4-5 minutes to complete this process. You're looking for this to really be almost a soft Nutella or peanut butter consistency. It should form a lovely rich chocolatey paste. Cover the bowl with clingfilm and set aside.

Whip the egg whites until they form soft peaks, then gradually add the remaining sugar. Keep whipping until it's smooth and incorporated. Fold in about a quarter of the chocolate paste and mix well, then fold in the rest. Keep it lovely and light.

Spoon the mix into the buttered ramekins and cook for 8–10 minutes until puffed up and cooked through. Serve with the confit.

RICE PUDDING
with fruit ripples

SERVES 4   PREPARATION TIME: 10 MINUTES   COOKING TIME: 30 MINUTES

As a kid we used to swirl jam through our rice pudding until it turned the whole thing pink. Instead of jam, I'm making a simple mixed berry compote – but you can still swirl it through the rice!

for the rice pudding
1 litre full-fat milk
500ml double cream
250g pudding rice
120g caster sugar
zest of ½ lemon or lime

zest of ½ orange
2 vanilla pods, sliced lengthways and seeds scraped (or 1 teaspoon vanilla extract)

for the fruit swirl
250g frozen mixed berries
3 tablespoons caster sugar

Place all the ingredients for the rice pudding in a heavy-based saucepan and slowly bring to the boil over a medium heat. Reduce the heat to low to medium and simmer for 25–30 minutes, giving it a stir every so often so that the rice doesn't stick to the bottom. The rice should be cooked, but with a little bite.

While it's cooking, tip the berries into a small bowl. Scatter over the sugar and pour in 100ml boiling water. Leave until the rice is ready.

Serve the creamy rice pudding in bowls and spoon the delicious freshly stewed berries over the top. Swirl through. Top with a little more orange or lime zest, if you like.

SARA LEE INSPIRED MANDARIN CHEESECAKE

SERVES 6   PREPARATION TIME: 20 MINUTES   CHILLING TIME: 30 MINUTES   COOKING TIME: 2 MINUTES

I've taken the best bits of this retro frozen dessert and mixed them up in a glass. The popping candy gives it an extra fizz and is a funny surprise for your guests at the end of the meal – you can leave it out if you like though.

3 mandarins
1 tablespoon caster sugar
1 teaspoon grated fresh root ginger
12 fresh mint leaves
a packet of popping candy (6 teaspoons)

for the cheesecake mix
180ml double cream
30ml crème fraîche
75g caster sugar
2 vanilla pods, split lengthways
  and seeds scraped
135g cream cheese

for the biscuit mix
25g butter
80g digestive biscuits (although
  I like to make this with Hobnobs)

Zest the mandarins into a bowl. Peel and segment the mandarin flesh and add to the bowl along with any juice. Scatter the sugar and ginger over the top and chill in the fridge for 30 minutes.

Whisk the cream, crème fraîche, sugar and vanilla seeds until thick. Add the cream cheese and continue to whisk until smooth and thick.

Melt the butter in a small pan and smash up the biscuits in a bowl. Pour the melted butter over the biscuits and stir until it just starts to come together in lovely buttery biscuit lumps.

Spoon the creamy mixture into small glass bowls, top with some of the biscuit mix and then scatter over the marinated mandarin segments. Tear 2 mint leaves on top of each pudding and finish with a teaspoon of delicious popping candy.

 JAM ROLY-POLY

SERVES 6   PREPARATION TIME: 45 MINUTES   CHILLING TIME: 30 MINUTES
COOKING TIME: 2–2½ HOURS

As kids, this always amazed us – how did the jam get *inside* the pudding? Now that we know how easy it is, there's no excuse for not making one. I've given instructions for steaming the pudding the old-fashioned way, but if you don't have a big enough steamer, you can do it in the oven (see the Tip for more info).

175g self-raising flour, plus extra to dust
1 teaspoon baking powder
a pinch of salt
150g vegetarian suet
100ml milk

5 tablespoons good-quality strawberry jam
a knob of butter, for greasing
1 x quantity of custard, to serve
 (see page 208)

Sift the flour, baking powder and salt into a bowl. Add the suet and use your fingertips to work it into a breadcrumb consistency. Slowly add the milk and mix together to form a soft, but not sticky dough – you may not need all the milk. Chill in the fridge for at least 30 minutes.

Warm the jam for 2 minutes in a small saucepan over a low heat. Meanwhile, lightly flour your work surface and roll your suet dough into a rectangle about the size of an A4 piece of paper and just under 1cm thick.

Spread the warm jam liberally over the surface, leaving a 1cm border all around the edge. Brush the edge with milk and roll up the suet dough from the long side, pinching the ends to seal in the jam.

Wrap the roly-poly loosely in buttered greaseproof paper and tie the ends with string like a Christmas cracker. Wrap it loosely again in foil, twisting the ends. Keep everything quite loose, as the pudding will puff up a bit as it cooks.

Steam over a saucepan of simmering water for 2–2½ hours – keep an eye on the water level and top up if you need to.

When cooked, carefully unwrap your pudding, slice and serve with plenty of warm custard.

TIP: *If your steamer isn't big enough, set a large roasting tin in the bottom of your oven with a wire rack directly above it. Fill it two-thirds full with kettle water and put the wrapped pudding on top. Cook at 180˚C for 1 hour.*

WELSH CAKES
with orange and basil mascarpone

SERVES 4–6 (MAKES 10)   PREPARATION TIME: 30 MINUTES   COOKING TIME: 6 MINUTES

This is my old cookery teacher's recipe and it's one of the first things I learned to cook. I'm serving it with a lovely orange and basil mascarpone, which I'm sure Miss will approve of! Thanks, Miss!

225g self-raising flour, plus extra to dust
75g caster sugar
½ teaspoon mixed spice
a pinch of salt
100g butter, cut into small pieces
50g currants
1 egg, beaten
a splash of milk

a little vegetable oil
1 teaspoon ground cinnamon
2 tablespoons sugar

for the orange and basil mascarpone
100g mascarpone
zest of 1 orange
1 tablespoon roughly chopped fresh basil

6cm cutter

Beat the mascarpone with the orange zest and basil until completely combined and smooth. Chill in the fridge while you make the Welsh cakes.

Tip the flour, sugar, mixed spice and salt into a bowl. Use your fingertips to rub in the butter until it has the consistency of breadcrumbs. Stir in the currants.

Add the egg and work into the mixture to form a fairly stiff dough – add a splash of milk if necessary to help bring it together.

Roll out the dough on a lightly floured work surface until it is about 5mm thick. Cut out rounds using a 6cm-cutter. You should get about 10.

Grease a flat griddle pan with a little oil and heat over a medium heat. Cook the Welsh cakes in batches, for 3 minutes on each side. Mix together the cinnamon and sugar and use it to dust the Welsh cakes just before serving with scoops of the mascarpone.

Welsh cakes are such a lovely thing to eat, especially when they're warm. Like any biscuit-type product, they're very moreish when they're hot out of the oven (or pan on this occasion!). I do have to say a big thanks to Miss for teaching me how to make these.

STORE CUPBOARD ESSENTIALS YOU CAN'T LIVE WITHOUT:

I am a great believer in using good-quality ingredients, but on a real budget there are some essentials I would recommend having in your store cupboard to make your life easier.

OILS
have a basic vegetable or rapeseed oil for cooking and then a good-quality olive oil for dressings, etc

BALSAMIC VINEGAR
ideal for dressings, roasting veg and sauces

MAYONNAISE, KETCHUP AND BROWN SAUCE
a burger and chips just isn't the same without these

WORCESTER SAUCE
a secret weapon in any-thing from a cheese toastie to a savoury bake

SOY SAUCE
light soy sauce is quite thin and has a saltier flavour, which works well in broths. Dark soy sauce is perfect for making marinades and dipping sauces

CAPERS AND OLIVES
fantastic for adding bursts of flavour

SUN-DRIED TOMATOES AND ARTICHOKES IN OIL
these are tasty in everything from risottos to salads and even the oil is full of flavour

SELECTION OF FLOURS
self-raising and plain flour are the most commonly used

ARBORIO RICE
risotto is a quick, simple, cost-effective but flavour-some dish when cooked well

PASTA
spaghetti and penne work well with almost any sauce

REFINED SUGAR
It is useful to have a variety in your cupboard, including Demerara, soft brown, white caster and icing sugar

STOCK CUBES
You can get very good quality stock cubes these days and they're always useful if you're in a hurry

DRIED CHILLIES
these really pack a punch so use with care!

SEA SALT AND TABLE SALT
the former can be a transformative seasoning while the latter dissolves easily so best for salting water

TINNED TUNA
you can buy surprisingly delicious tinned tuna in supermarkets, save the oil it comes in and use in a sauce or dressing

BAR OF DECENT CHOCOLATE
the benefits of chocolate containing a minimum of 70% cocoa solids has long been reputed and you will notice the difference in your cooking and baking

DIJON MUSTARD
this will add a kick to your hot dog or burger

DRIED OREGANO
the only dried herb that is really worth using

LEMON JUICE
if fresh lemons aren't something you can stock, a bottle of lemon juice can be just as helpful

OILS AND SALAD DRESSINGS

Making your own flavoured oils and vinegars is really easy to do, and the results taste amazing. They're great for livening up salad dressings and also for dipping bread into, or for drizzling over cooked meat.

Here are some of my favourites:

ROSEMARY OIL:

You'll need a bottle of good-quality olive oil and three sprigs of fresh rosemary, washed and thoroughly dried. Gently bruise the rosemary between your palms, and add it to the olive oil (you may need to pour out a little of the oil to make room for the herbs). Seal the bottle tightly, give it a good shake, then leave in a cool, dark place for a week or two. This is also delicious if you crush a couple of garlic cloves in the oil, but if you do, store the oil in the fridge and don't keep it for more than a couple of days.

CHILLI OIL:

Empty the contents of a good-quality olive oil into a saucepan and add a tablespoon of dried chilli flakes and 3 or 4 whole dried chillies. Bring the pan to a simmer, then remove from the heat. When it has cooled slightly, pour the oil and chilli mixture back into the bottle. Seal tightly and leave in a cool, dark place for a few weeks to develop its heat and flavour. It will get hotter the longer you leave it.

LEMON OIL:

Finely grate the zest from three unwaxed lemons. Add the zest to a bottle of good-quality olive oil, shake well and leave to sit for a couple of weeks. After that time, sieve the oil to remove the bits of zest, then place back in the bottle to enjoy whenever you like. This is one best kept in the fridge, to preserve the delicate flavour.

TARRAGON VINEGAR:

Start with a bottle of the best-quality white wine vinegar you can find. You'll also need about 3 tablespoons of tarragon, leaves picked off the stems. Gently bruise the leaves between your palms before adding them to the vinegar. Give the mixture a good shake and leave in a cool, dark place to infuse. After two weeks, strain the vinegar to remove the tarragon leaves, then pour the flavoured vinegar back into the cleaned bottle. This looks beautiful if you put a fresh sprig of tarragon into the bottle.

FRENCH DRESSING:

Measure 1 part vinegar to 3 parts oil into a bowl or jar with a teaspoon of Dijon mustard. Season with salt and pepper and shake well to combine. You can experiment with the quantities of oil and vinegar to find what you like best. It is delicious made with tarragon vinegar or with very finely chopped fresh herbs.

BALSAMIC DRESSING:

This is a really simple and tasty dressing. Just mix 1 tablespoon of balsamic vinegar with 3 tablespoons of olive oil and some salt and pepper to season. Just try it on French beans – it is truly amazing.

KITCHEN EQUIPMENT

I don't tend to use overly fancy equipment. I cook in a fairly traditional way, which doesn't require anything too scientific and brain teasing. To get you through this book and set your home kitchen up well, here are a few things to get you started – 'the essentials'.

A COUPLE OF FRYING PANS
one small and one large

A GOOD SELECTION OF SAUCEPANS

ROASTING DISHES

BLENDER
a food processor can make your life in the kitchen so much easier. I use mine for blitzing sauces, soups, shakes and dressings

KNIVES
straight-edged cook's knife
paring knife
good serrated knife
bread knife
kitchen scisssors

TONGS

WOODEN SPOON

ROLLING PIN

SPATULA

WHISK

A COUPLE OF CHOPPING BOARDS
plastic and wooden

MEASURING JUG

PEELER

GRATER

A SELECTION OF MIXING BOWLS

TIMER

SIEVE

COLANDER

LEMON SQUEEZER

POTATO MASHER

CAN OPENER

SALAD SPINNER

WIRE COOLING-RACK

LADLE

MY FAVOURITE PLACES TO

EAT AND DRINK

DUCK & WAFFLE
Heron Tower, City of London

Dan Doherty is a bloody brilliant chef and creates the most amazing combinations. Plus the view is very special.

BURGER & LOBSTER
Soho, London

What a great idea – love this place!

PICCOLINO
Chester

Most Mondays I have dinner here before heading out to party with friends.

MARLOW BAR AND GRILL
Marlow

When at Luke's Dining Room, this is my local. The tandoori sea bass is amazing.

SIAM THAI AND TEPPANYAKI
Chester

'Steve Siam' is one of the loveliest guys in the world – he runs such a great place!

MUDDY DUCK PUB
Hethe, Oxfordshire

My good friend Nigel Harris runs this place – the best fish stew in the world.

WAGAMAMA

Chicken katsu curry – number 71, I think. Just utterly brilliant.

BRASSERIE ZÉDEL
London

Such good value for really lovely food.

THE IMPERIAL
King's Road, London

Delicious food and a great spot for people-watching.

PATTY & BUN
James Street, London

They make the most incredible burgers from fresh, carefully sourced ingredients. Fabulous.

HUNAN
Pimlico Road, London

This place is amazing. They don't have a menu – you just tell them what you do and don't like and they take care of the rest.

CRUISE NIGHTCLUB
Chester

Since turning eighteen, I have spent pretty much every Monday night at my friends' student night, 'Beans', at this club. It's a great place for me to go and relax and have fun with my close friends.

SHOP

HAWARDEN ESTATE FARM SHOP
Flintshire, Wales

As a kid I used to go and pick my own fruit and veg here, it's transformed into a food-lovers heaven now. A must for all foodies.

BARBECOA BUTCHERY
Watling Street, London

This is such a cool butcher's shop – some of the best meat you'll ever taste.

TURNER & GEORGE
St John Street, London

This is an incredible old-school butcher's shop and well worth a visit, but if you can't make it to Clerkenwell, they have a great website.

MY THOUGHTS ON WINE

Many people are put off and intimidated by the snobbery associated with wines. There are so many different countries producing wine and each of those countries, it would seem, has a huge number of styles, regions, grapes, and so on. Most wines are better with food – next time you have some wine with your dinner, try tasting the wine before eating and then try with your food – the difference can be astounding.

You could drag out a few dusty tomes, roll up your sleeves and embark on a crash course on all things wine. This is great if you have endless amounts of free time and a bottomless pit of money but if not, hopefully this short guide will help you to enjoy wine as much as I do!

My recommendation is that, to get the best possible value, you should be spending about £8 as a minimum. I would also recommend buying wines from places that are not the best known and not from the better-known brands – you are always paying a premium for this. If you really like Pinot Grigio try a different white from Italy – you will be surprised and delighted. If you are big fan of Rioja try something else from Spain at the same price – you will be amazed.

When it comes to matching food and wine there are no hard and fast rules. Despite popular ideas on the subject there are plenty of red wines that go beautifully with some types of fish dishes and, conversely, there are some white wines that are ideal with some meat dishes! With the combination of food and wine the thing to consider is balance. An oily dish will often benefit from something crisp with high acidity. A spicy curry with an off-dry, crisp Riesling is a heaven-sent combo. A big, powerful beef stew can be balanced with the lovely sweet fruited flavours of Pinot Noir. Boeuf Bourguignon and a red Burgundy such as Gevrey Chambertin is a classic example of this winning combination. In most European countries you will find that the local wine and cuisine go hand in hand. Be brave and experiment. One of the greatest food and wine partnerships I have ever tried is blue cheese with a very sweet, late harvest wine – try them both separately and then together – absolute heaven! (Port and Stilton is traditional and a lovely, heady combination).

When talking to people about wine, I am often told that they like Rioja or Merlot or Shiraz and sometimes people will state with absolute certainty that, 'I don't like French (Italian, Australian, South African or whichever country's wines they have taken a dislike to) wine.' These are nothing more than prejudices acquired due to not being exposed to a wide enough choice of that country's wines – nothing more! If you enjoy wine then you will find a wine you like from any of the main wine-producing countries.

Over the page is a list of wines that go beautifully with some of my signature dishes but you could try these with similar recipes from this book or elsewhere.

RED MEAT

VENISON BURGER (page 72)
Gerard Bertrand, Chateau La Sauvageonne,
Coteaux du Languedoc – France 2010

This is a lovely rich, spicy, smooth red from the sunny South of France. The classic smoky, black pepper and earthy red fruit flavours of the main grape used in this wine, the Syrah (aka Shiraz) grape really complements the gamey nature of the Venison. A rugged wine, with flavours of the wild (Sauvage) country-side nearby.

GLAZED PORK RIBS (page 87)
Carmen Reserva, Pinot Noir,
Leyda – Chile 2012

With the sweet sticky sauce you will need a full-bodied wine with lovely sweet fruit and low tannins (the part of the wine that can give the wine a hard, dry taste). New World Pinot Noir fits the bill.

LUXURY STEAK (page 89)
Andeluna, 'Altitud' Malbec,
Uco Valley – Argentina 2011

Steak and Malbec is the match! This intense, perfumed wine from the foothills of the Andes is a perfect choice. It's a beast of a wine with huge fruity flavours and a brooding magnificence.

SPAGHETTI BOLOGNESE (page 108)
Casa Delle Valle 'El Tidon',
Cabernet Sauvignon Tempranillo,
Tierra da Castilla – Spain 2012

This fabulous, richly fruited and robust, oaked red has all the guts to stand up to a hearty pasta dish like this. Coming from one of Spain's emerging regions it offers Rioja-like sweet, smoky fruit at fantastic value for money.

BREADED LAMB CUTLETS (page 133)
Pérez Cruz, Cabernet Sauvignon Reserva,
Alto Maipo Valley – Chile 2011

This wine has an intense rosemary and eucalyptus flavour alongside the full-throttle black-currant fruit of the Cabernet Sauvignon grape. A really juicy red wine with enough soft tannin and good acidity to cut through the fat in the lamb.

PAN-FRIED PORK CHOPS WITH BLACK PUDDING CROQUETTES (page 130)
Domaine de la Ville Rouge, Crozes-
Hermitage, 'Terre d'Eclat', Rhone – France

The richness of black pudding in this dish cries out for a classic Syrah from the northern Rhone. The wine is packed with smoky red fruits, herbs and undergrowth.

WHITE MEAT

CHICKEN BREASTS WRAPPED IN BACON (page 100)
Domaine René Monnier, Meursault, 'Le
Limozin', Burgundy – France 2011

A classic combination. The subtle smoky butteriness and streak of minerality in this wine works incredibly well with the soft, subtle flavours of the chicken.

FISH

LOBSTER FISHFINGER SANDWICH (page 78)

Gaia 'Wild Ferment', Assyrtiko, Santorini – Greece 2012

Stunning intense, smoky, salty, mineral-laden white from Santorini that is a brilliant match. One of the most intense white wines on the planet. This is about as far from Retsina or Domestica as you can get!

GRILLED SALMON WITH LETTUCE, CUCUMBER AND TOMATO (page 175)

Schloss Johannisberg, Riesling QbA 'Yellow Label', Rheingau – Germany 2012

The beautiful, taught precision of this German Riesling is as good as it gets. It is produced on one of the oldest wine estates in the world – you cannot get more retro than that!

ROASTED COD IN PARSLEY SAUCE (page 117)

Castello di Pomino, Pomino Bianco, Pomino, Tuscany – Italy 2011

The classic, subtle flavours of this dish cry out for an intense but subtle wine. This aristocratic Tuscan white complements but does not overwhelm the dish.

SMOKED HADDOCK AND CRAB CAKES (page 118)

Larry Cherubino, Ad Hoc, 'Hen and Chicken,' Chardonnay, Pemberton – Western Australia

A beautifully balanced Chardonnay packed with fruit with a lovely smoky edge to complement the smokiness in the haddock.

SURF AND TURF (page 172)

Remoissenet Pere et Fils, Nuits-St-Georges, 1er Cru, Burgundy – France 2009

Pinot Noir is probably the greatest grape at walking the flavour tightrope between seafood and steak. This is a classic example.

VEGGIE

GNOCCHI WITH WILD MUSHROOM RAGU (page 176)

Marchesi de Frescobaldi, Castello di Nipozzano, Chianti Rufina Riserva, Tuscany – Italy 2009

What else but classic Chianti! Bitter-sweet cherries with layers of blackcurrant jam and wood-smoke. A wine with an incredible pedigree.

PEA AND GOAT'S CHEESE RISOTTO (page 138)

Woollaston Sauvignon Blanc, Nelson – New Zealand 2012

Sauvignon Blanc is the perfect white wine with goat's cheese. The very intense mineral and pea-pod flavours of Nelson Sauvignon consummate the relationship (nudge-nudge).

≡ INDEX ≡

THANKS

There are so many people who have supported me up to this stage in my career and I have been overwhelmed by the continued encouragement, but I really do owe some super-special thanks to these guys:

My mum, Debbie, for always being there for me and being so supportive; my dad and especially my wonderful nan who inspired me to start cooking in the first place, plus a special thanks to the whole family for their support.

Steve Vaughan for spending so much time with me at such an early age helping with my butchery skills, Danny Burke for his support and helping me through my cooking competitions. Dan Hunter and the guys at Soughton Hall who I worked with during my early teens, before Dan then taught me at Yale College in Wrexham. Also thanks to Simon Radley at The Chester Grosvenor.

None of this would have happened without support from Connah's Quay High School. Mary Richmond, my cookery teacher, was so encouraging throughout every single stage and even to this day, 'Miss' is always at the end of the phone when I need her advice. Also all of my friends at High School – I don't get to see them as much as I'd like, but I still keep in touch with most of them. I wouldn't be a twenty-year-old without a bit of partying so thanks to Cruise, Chester for looking after me and all the great people I enjoy a night off with every Monday.

Brian Turner and the Springboard Charity have continued to help ever since I won FutureChef in 2009. Brian is one of the loveliest guys in the world and is always there to keep an eye on how things are going. Thanks also to the rest of the wonderful team.

Iain Donald and the team at IRC: James, Antonio, Adam and many more, but Iain has been one of the biggest influences on my career so far. Plus the restaurants and hotels around the world that took me under their wing for a short time whilst I was on my year of work-experience placements.

Don and Judy for their overwhelming kindness over the past few years from our holidays to cheering on the Reds!

Mark Fuller gave me the opportunity of a lifetime at the age of eighteen to open Luke's Dining Room in Berkshire. Mark became a real mentor and close personal friend of mine. A special mention also to Terry and Colin for also supporting me through every moment, plus the tremendous team behind the scenes, and the team at Luke's Broadway for doing a brilliant job.

And now, to the guys at Penguin who have worked on this book with me: Lindsey, John, Sarah, Tamsin, Beatrix, Laura, Alison. Also, Daniel O'Keefe who has helped to build my small knowledge of wine, and Chris Terry and Rick Barrett.

There are so many more to mention, but I would like thank you all for your love and support throughout this journey. xx